D0639365

Ninety Days

Resources for Lent and Eastertime in the RCIA

Edited by
Karan Hinman Powell
and Joseph P. Sinwell

PAULIST PRESS
New York/Mahwah, N.J.

ALSO EDITED BY KARAN H. POWELL AND JOSEPH P. SINWELL
PUBLISHED BY PAULIST PRESS

Breaking Open the Word of God (Cycle A)
Breaking Open the Word of God (Cycle B)
Breaking Open the Word of God (Cycle C)
(*Resources for Using the Lectionary for Catechesis in the RCIA*)

Excerpts from the English translation of *The Roman Missal* © 1973, International Committee on English in the Liturgy, Inc. All rights reserved.

Library of Congress Cataloging-in-Publication Data

Ninety days: resources for Lent and Eastertime in the RCIA/edited
  by Karan H. Powell and Joseph P. Sinwell.
     p.   cm.
  Includes bibliographical references.
  ISBN 0-8091-3110-2
  1. Catholic Church. Ordo initiationis Christianae adultorum.
  2. Initiation rites—Religious aspects—Catholic Church—Liturgy.
  3. Catholic Church—Membership. 4. Christian education of adults.
  5. Catechumens—Religious life. 6. Christian life—Catholic
authors. 7. Lent. 8. Eastertide. I. Powell, Karan H. (Karan
Hinman), 1953– . II. Sinwell, Joseph P. III. Title: 90 days.
BX2045.I553N56   1989
268'.434—dc20
                                          89–37640
                                             CIP

Published by Paulist Press
997 Macarthur Boulevard
Mahwah, New Jersey 07430

Printed and bound in the
United States of America

Contents

Dedication

In gratitude for their inspiration, faith and love

Mrs. Mary Buretz
Sarah E. S. Sinwell
Benjamin J. Sinwell
Luke E. Sinwell

Introduction

Breaking Open the Word: Resources Using the Lectionary for Cate-chesis in the RCIA for Cycles A, B, and C published by Paulist Press presented catechetical sessions based on the lectionary to be used during the catechumenate period. This book focuses on the periods of purification and enlightenment (Lent) and mystagogia (the Easter season) and is an extension of those first three books. Like *Breaking Open the Word,* this book is a tool to assist catechists and mystagogues in preparation for Sunday catechetical sessions.

In this book you will find outlines for catechetical sessions for Cycle A readings for Lent as well as session outlines for Cycles A, B, and C for the Easter season. Why only Cycle A for Lent? Only Cycle A readings are used for the celebration of the rite of election and scrutinies whenever there are candidates for initiation at the Easter vigil. While Cycle A is the preferred cycle for use with the neophytes, this book has diverged from this prefer-ence by offering sample session outlines for mystagogical sessions using Cycles B and C readings.

The use of these outlines presumes:

1. That the elect are separate from those who are still inquirers or cate-chumens.
2. That the elect are now proceeding to the celebration of the Easter sacraments and will celebrate the rites of election, scrutiny, baptism, first eucharist, and confirmation during these ninety days.
3. That the parish celebrates the scrutinies.
4. That the parish celebrates the rite of dismissal for all the elect and candidates for full communion in a eucharistic liturgy.
5. That candidates and elect participate in the diocesan rite of election.
6. That the Easter vigil is alive and rich with full symbol (lots of water, bread, wine, oil) so that these symbols speak to the neophytes and offer content for the period of mystagogia.
7. That the parish catechumenate team promotes the principles of adult religious education in the catechumenate.
8. That Lent is a time of intense spiritual formation.
9. That elect and neophytes, as well as team members, have available their own copy of the scriptures during each of these sessions.
10. That these sessions are to be a "model" and are not to be duplicated verbatim unless they so fit a particular parish!

Although this volume is primarily intended for use in parish catechumenates, a variety of pastoral ministers could easily adapt it—for personal reflection, for parish Lenten retreats and Lenten programs modeled after the Lenten sessions contained herein, for scripture sharing and post-RENEW processes which use the mystagogia sessions as stepping stones to explore their own on-going mystagogia, the breaking open of the mysteries of their life in faith as Catholic Christians.

We wish to acknowledge the contributing authors for their cooperation and creativity: Mr. Robert Hamma of Paulist Press for his support and encouragement through all four books, our families for enabling us to make time and space to do the work required to complete each book, and our friends and colleagues who have given us the inspiration and direction we have needed.

Victoria M. Tufano

The Rites of Lent

In the cool dampness of a spring night, the church gathers to do once again what people have done since the beginning of time: to light fires against the darkness, to remember the stories of our origins, to initiate new members, to share a sacred meal, and to remember who we are.

For the faithful, the Easter vigil is a milestone along the journey of faith, a time to shake loose the dust of the road and to be bathed once more in the light and the water. For the elect it is the night of final passage. It sums up all the previous rites of passage, both the formal, ritualized ones provided by the church, and the small, personal moments of passage that have led to this point.

From this night on the elect will continue the journey as full members, partners in the mission of Christ's church. On this night the elect are asked six questions:

Do you reject Satan?
And all his works?
And all his empty promises?

Do you believe in God the Father . . . ?
Do you believe in Jesus Christ . . . ?
Do you believe in the Holy Spirit . . . and the life everlasting?

With these six questions, and six repeated "I do's," celebrated in their fullness with the ancient signs of water, oil, bread, and wine, the elect commit themselves to a covenant with the redeeming, life-giving and ever-loving God.

This covenant commits them to faithfulness in situations as yet unknown; it frees them to reject temptations as yet unoffered; it asks them to answer "I do" to questions as yet unasked. The faithful who witness the elect entering into this covenant will recommit themselves to it later in the liturgy. But even they, having lived in this covenant since their own bap-

3

tisms, cannot say what it will yet require of them. Such is the nature of a covenant relationship.

The period of purification and enlightenment provides a time of interior reflection for the elect to prepare themselves to enter into this covenant. This time "is intended to purify the minds and hearts of the elect as they search their own consciences and do penance. This period is intended as well to enlighten the minds and hearts of the elect with a deeper knowledge of Christ the Savior." (RCIA 139) The primary vehicles for purification and enlightenment are the rites of scrutiny and the presentations.

The Scrutinies

The scrutinies are ordinarily celebrated within the Sunday assembly on the Third, Fourth, and Fifth Sundays of Lent. The readings for these celebrations are those of Year A; ritual masses for the scrutinies are provided in the sacramentary under "Christian Initiation: The Scrutinies."

The scrutinies afford the elect, and, indeed, the entire assembly, the opportunity to examine their own hearts and minds by the light of the gospel. The ability of the elect to engage in such self-searching at the scrutinies rests largely upon their having learned to do so during the period of catechumenate. The gradual transformation or conversion engendered by the word of God during the catechumenate is deepened by the celebration of the scrutinies.

The focus of the scrutinies is "to uncover, then heal all that is weak, defective, or sinful in the hearts of the elect; to bring out, then strengthen all that is upright, strong, and good. For the scrutinies are celebrated in order to deliver the elect from the power of sin and Satan, to protect them against temptation, and to give them strength in Christ, who is the way, the truth, and the life." (RCIA 141) By means of the scrutinies, the elect are gradually taught to perceive sin and evil in their various aspects, and to repent of them.

The first scrutiny focuses primarily on the individual aspect of sin. The liturgy of the word centers around the gospel of the Samaritan woman at the well (Jn 4:5–42). In her bantering dialogue with Jesus, the woman asks for the living water he promises. Her motivation for this request is quite mundane; she would prefer not to have to draw water from the well each day. Her presence at the well at mid-day suggests her reluctance to socialize with the other women of the town who would be drawing their families' water supply in the cool of early morning. When Jesus touches upon the cause of this isolation from the life of the community, she neatly manages to change the subject to something safer: theological debate. Even so, Jesus is able to reveal himself to the woman, and she calls the rest of the townsfolk to hear him.

The story suggests that the woman's isolation and her desire for a water which will never cause her to thirst again are the result of her own sin. In choosing to have numerous husbands and other men, she has put herself outside the life of the community. Although the gospel doesn't resolve her living situation, it does put her back into the community as a result of accepting Jesus as the messiah.

The second scrutiny focuses primarily on the social aspect of sin. The gospel of the man born blind (Jn 9:1–41) asks the community to reflect not so much on the physical healing of the blind man as on his gradually growing insight concerning Jesus. At the same time, the gospel reveals the growing blindness of those around the formerly blind man who refuse to receive the vision that he tries to share with them. Jesus names as the sinners in this story those who choose blindness and then call it sight in order to maintain their own positions.

While the gospel invites its hearers to look within for the blindness of sin in their individual lives, it also deepens their awareness of the social aspects of sin. By virtue of their participation in the life of the world, the elect participate in the communal and systemic sins which permeate it. The second scrutiny calls upon the elect to see these sins, and to repent of them. As Christians they seek to stop cooperating with the blindness that the world calls light: with the powers of the world refusing to see homeless people, and then declaring that there are none; with women and minorities being harassed in the workplace, and then being called equal; with implements of destruction being named peacekeepers; with lying as a matter of corporate policy; with the unborn being sacrificed in the name of quality of life; with any lie, injustice, or secret which is carried out in the name of any good.

The final scrutiny calls upon the elect to examine "the death-dealing power of the spirit of evil" (RCIA 175A) and to recognize the power of Christ to free them and all creation from death. It prepares them to participate in the Christian mission to announce and live the kingdom of God by arming them with the knowledge that there are other kingdoms seeking power and claiming sovereignty. In baptism they will renounce Satan, his works, and his promises; this scrutiny most clearly exposes his works and promises. His works and his promises are death. The third scrutiny names the demons of materialism, racism, sexism, militarism, nationalism, addictions to substances and behaviors, and other powers which claim dominion over human life and proclaims the power of Jesus Christ to subdue them.

Each scrutiny includes intercessions for the elect which permit the community to name the sins and evils that are being committed to the power of God. The intercessions given in the text, like those given in the sacramentary and other ritual books, are samples, guidelines for the composition of intercessions that reflect the situation of the community which prays them. In the case of the scrutinies, the intercession for the elect must reflect the struggles against the sins which the community identifies as being present within it. Those who compose these intercessions must know both the elect and the entire parish community.

These intercessions serve to name the demons, to bring them into the light. Having done this, the church calls upon God to free, heal, and protect the elect that they may worship in truth, witness to the faith, and live in the glory of the resurrection.

The three scrutinies together prepare the elect to answer the first three questions to be asked of them at the Easter vigil: "Do you renounce Satan? And all his works? And all his empty promises?" Even after their baptism, they will continue to be confronted by Satan, his works, and his promises. They will continue to be tempted by the easy, the false, and the seemingly glamorous life that sin can offer. But they will have come to recognize these things for what they are, and to know that the power of God can and will overcome them.

For these elect, and for all the faithful, the celebration of the scrutinies in subsequent Lents will offer them the opportunity to prepare to celebrate the Easter vigil. These celebrations will call them to reflect upon the sins and weaknesses which have caused them to fall short of their baptismal commitments. The scrutinies invite the faithful to celebrate God's continuing power over sin in their lives by taking part in the sacrament of penance.

Finally, the scrutinies present the elect with images and symbols that will figure heavily in the Easter vigil. The images of water, light, and new life will recur throughout the vigil readings, and again in the liturgy of baptism. These images and the scriptures which contain them provide a language for the newly baptized to use in unlocking the mystery of baptism in the period of mystagogy.

The Presentations

Interspersed among the three scrutinies are the rites of the presentation of the creed and of the Lord's prayer. These two rites publicly celebrate the handing on of the tradition of faith and prayer to the elect by the community.

The rite of presentation of the creed usually takes place during the third week of Lent, at a weekday celebration of the eucharist, or at some other parish liturgical celebration. The readings for this rite (Lectionary 748) provide a meditation on faith and the profession of faith. Along with the Israelites, the faithful and the elect are admonished to believe in the Lord and to take their faith into all aspects of their lives. The various other readings provided as options for this rite repeat the promise that those who profess faith in Christ will be saved.

The rubric for the homily (RCIA 159) instructs the celebrant to explain "the meaning and importance of the creed in relation to the teaching that the elect have already received and to the profession of faith that they must make at their baptism and uphold throughout their lives." This rubric points to the fact that this celebration is an act of ritual catechesis. It calls to mind the formation which has already taken place, and provides the great symbol of the creed for the faith as professed and lived.

The rite of presentation of the creed most clearly expresses that it is the community of faith which hands on the tradition. The actual presentation is the community's profession of the creed in the presence of the elect. This is the first time, the rite presumes, that the elect are present for the recitation of the creed.

The community hands on the creed with the expectation that the elect will learn it by heart. The preparation rites for Holy Saturday morning provide an opportunity for the elect to "give back" the creed by reciting it from memory. More importantly, the elect will publicly commit themselves to professing the creed with their lives as they are baptized.

From the time they are baptized, they will stand with the community at its Sunday gathering and profess the creed in response to the proclamation of the word of God. Just as the rite of acceptance into the order of catechumens admitted them to the hearing of the word, with which they were then dismissed, so, in a sense, their profession of faith admits them to the proclamation of the creed. When they are dismissed, they will now carry the creed into the world with them. By presenting the elect with the creed, the church is entrusting to them their role in its mission of proclaiming its faith to the world.

The custom of presenting the elect with a scroll inscribed with the creed seems to have become a permanent fixture in the celebration of this rite. While a beautifully illuminated manuscript of the creed is certainly a fitting addition to a Christian home, it must be noted that the giving of such a scroll is not what is meant by a "presentation." The act of handing over this object must not be allowed to overshadow the community's action of handing on the creed verbally. This may mean that the scroll is given after the elect are dismissed. It certainly means that the community's recitation of the creed must be done in a deliberate manner.

Rather than the race to "life everlasting. Amen" that characterizes many a Sunday morning creed, this presentation must have the character of the giving of a precious family heirloom. This may be accomplished by inviting the community to repeat the creed in segments after the presider, or, perhaps, by having a sung acclamation interspersed throughout the creed, such as the one found in David Haas' collection *Who Calls You By Name*. May such care for the creed as it is presented in this rite eventually spill over into the Sunday liturgy!

In the fifth week of Lent, the church presents to the elect the Lord's prayer. Like the presentation of the creed, the presentation of the Lord's prayer is preferably celebrated in the midst of the parish community.

The options for the first two readings provided for this rite (Lectionary 749) invite the community to ponder the image of God as Father. In the reading from the prophet Hosea, the Lord speaks as one who teaches a child to walk, who presses a child to his cheek, and who stoops to feed him. This tender image is echoed in the shepherd of Psalm 23 and the father of Psalm 103. The two Pauline readings reflect on the presence of the Spirit of the Son within us, making us adopted children who cry out to "Abba" (Papa) as only a child and heir could.

After the second reading, the elect are called forward to hear the gospel reading. In this rite it is Christ himself, present in the proclamation of the gospel, who teaches the elect to pray as he taught his disciples. Note that the gospel reading as it appears in the Lectionary is different from the way it appears in the rite. The translation in the rite uses the traditional Catholic form of the prayer; the one who is to proclaim the gospel should be aware of this.

The homilist is entrusted with the task of explaining both the prayer itself and the place the prayer has in the life of the baptized. The prayer, whether recited alone or with others, always places the Christian in the community of the baptized. It is always prayed in the plural, and it exercises the privilege of those who have received the Spirit of God the Son in baptism to address the Father of Jesus as their Father. The elect will not pray this prayer publicly until they have been baptized and take their place at the community's celebration of the eucharist.

This prayer forms the heart of the church's tradition of prayer. It places the Christian in right relationship with God. Those who pray this prayer look to God for all their needs, seek to do the will of the Father, look forward to the coming of God's kingdom, seek to forgive and to be forgiven, and look for deliverance from evil. In other words, those who pray this way seek to live as those who have been rescued from the sin of Adam and Eve. From the earliest years of the church, it has been a central element in the morning and evening prayers of Christians. Since the fourth century, it has been included in the communion rite of the mass.

For those about to be baptized, this prayer contains within it all that they need to know about living life in Christ. It offers a model for their relationship with God in Christ. Because of this relationship, initiated by God, fostered by the ministry of the faith community, nourished by the gospel, and purified by prayer and repentance, the elect can commit themselves to a covenant which commits them to faithfulness in situations as yet unknown, frees them to reject temptations as yet unoffered, asks them to answer "I do" to questions as yet unasked.

Thomas J. Caroluzza

Neophytes and
the Easter Season

Are you having difficulty knowing what to do after the Easter vigil? If you answer "yes," you are in good company. If you answer "no," you may be in big trouble. Most catechumenal teams throughout the United States are dissatisfied with their practice of mystagogy. We are not happy with what we're doing with the neophytes during the Easter season, but this is not a new problem. Those who have been into the catechumenate for fourteen years—let's call them the founding mothers and fathers of the catechumenate in America—have been experimenting with mystagogy annually, and to date I haven't met any who would hold up their pastoral practice as a model to be emulated. Let's admit it—we're all striving to be mystagogues and none of us has made it yet.

In recent times I've begun my workshops by asking the participants to name the key issues of mystagogy. I have not been surprised by the responses. Everywhere there is talk of "a letdown" after the vigil. Someone said recently: "The whole thing seems to fizzle like one of those fireworks in the midst of a Fourth-of-July display. It all begins with great promise and excitement but it never quite delivers the expected impact." Several participants in the workshop felt that they had to be doing something wrong, and one was candid enough to admit that in his parish mystagogy was ignored altogether. A few of them said they were not certain about what it is that they should be doing during this period. And, as you might have guessed, someone spoke out for many in calling for some models to help everyone know what to do.

We all have a penchant for taking the short cut by borrowing good ideas and practical suggestions that work somewhere else. In the workshop there was a pervasive sentiment that if mystagogy is as essential to the initiation process as everyone makes it out to be, it shouldn't be so difficult to implement. And, of course, there was someone who suspected that mystagogy was an antiquarian transplant from a former age and would never take hold in twentieth century America. The few at our workshops

10

who had implemented some program during the fifty days surfaced their own brand of issues: One felt that mystagogy was important to prevent dropouts, and another was concerned that the three sessions offered in their parish had no impact on the people in the pews.

The bottom line from all these responses was that we are all having a difficult time with mystagogy. Without statistical support, we can be fairly certain that our efforts to implement mystagogy fall within the range of non-practice, little practice and malpractice. It is an understatement to suggest that for most parish catechumenal teams and for most neophytes, mystagogy is not a very satisfying experience.

I am convinced that our problems with this fourth and final period of the initiation process lie in our inability to name and understand clearly the unique and distinguishing character of mystagogy. It is not just about making more time for the catechesis we couldn't fit into our truncated catechumenate period. It is not merely a program to ensure that we don't lose those who were initiated at the vigil. It is not a pastoral ploy to keep the catechumenal team busy until we can gear up for the next group of inquirers. No, mystagogy is an essential element of the initiatory experience.

It is a distinct period with its own unique goals. It cannot be ignored, omitted or treated lightly, for it is the natural consequence of the entire catechumenal process. And for all these reasons, it demands the special skills of a gifted and trained mystagogue.

So where do we begin if we hope to develop a better understanding of this period of the catechumenate and an effective practice that flows from that understanding? There is certainly some wisdom in knowing the history of this period, but I would not recommend that as an approach to our present understanding of mystagogy. A study of the mystagogical catechesis of Cyril of Jerusalem, for instance, will certainly help us understand the importance of sacramental catechesis during this period, but I do not believe that knowledge will translate into an effective pastoral practice. Or, to take another example, the reading of Egeria's observations while on her pilgrimage to Jerusalem may enlighten us about the necessity for a time of retreat and reflection during the octave, but I do not think that knowledge will drive us to design an eight day experience with the bishop or pastor before Low Sunday.[1] Nor do I feel that a thorough study of the introduction to our revised and present rite will yield the inspiration that will prompt us to an authentic practice of mystagogy in our time. Certainly we need to be familiar with the eight paragraphs which describe mystagogy in the rite, but one soon becomes aware that less space is devoted to mystagogy than any other period of the catechumenate, and what is said is so broad-stroked that it offers little help with understanding or pastoral practice.

It has been my experience that the best route into a more complete understanding of mystagogy and its consequent practice is to help people identify some mystagogical experiences from their non-ecclesial lives. I like to send them outside the church setting to discover the importance of this period. When people are able to name their human experiences, they come to lasting insights about this period. Admittedly, this is an end-run approach, but I feel it gets us to the goal more quickly. If people can name moments when they felt they were in touch with a mystery, a heightened experience that filled them with awe and wonder, a time of breathtaking insight or breakthrough realization, then it will be fairly easy for them to identify some mystagogical aspect to that experience. Once that is accomplished, making the connection to the fourth period is a piece of cake. This is an attempt to disengage them temporarily from the Easter mysteries in order to return with a new language and a common experience that helps interpret mystagogy in new ways. This approach allows people to get the smell of mystagogy, a pervasive feel for it, a comfort with it, a sense of the period before they attempt to define it or develop a pastoral practice for it. This approach demystifies mystagogia. That may be the greatest need at the parish level these days if we hope to develop an effective pastoral practice.

What I would suggest as a first step is that every catechumenal team go out and rent the video of "Swimming to Cambodia." This may seem like an unlikely source, but I think it will massage the team into the spirit of mystagogy. Those of you who have already seen the film will recall that the comedian (read "Mystagogue"), sitting behind a plain desk, and with a seventy-five cent notebook before him, and one of those pull-down screens you can find in any elementary school, plays out for us one of the most riveting stream-of-consciousness unpackings of a thirty second heightened experience I have ever viewed. I won't ruin it for you by telling all the details (you have to experience it to know it). It is enough to say that one gets a sense of what mystagogy is all about in the viewing. The comedian accordions out a brief experience off the coast of Thailand into split-second frames. But what we get as viewers is an exploration of a very dense and unitive moment of his life. What he has done is real mystagogy. He has explored the deep layers of memory that were touched off by his experience. There is nothing so compelling as to view such moments being unraveled. That is what mystagogia is all about. It is an attempt to articulate some brief moment, some personal earthquake that shifted the subterranean layers of one's soul or cracked one's civilized veneer. The telling in "Swimming to Cambodia" had for me all the spontaneous exuberance, all the enthusiastic gutsiness of a secular mystagogy, a knock-your-socks-off, experiential catechesis on the springs of living water.[2]

After viewing this film I would suggest that all present get in touch with some heightened experience in their lives. These will become analogues for mystagogy.

When I have done this, the most frequently mentioned experience is that of love. Encouraged to play out the process, people will name the dating experience, falling in love, a courting period that leads to a decision for marriage, the preparation for and celebration of a wedding, and the honeymoon. This common human experience helps them situate mystagogy as an essential element in the catechumenal process. It is fairly easy to draw out the connections and the insights gained from this exercise. Like the honeymoon, it is necessary to retreat after the vigil experience. This is a time for remembering, a time of discovery, a time for reflecting back on the celebration. It is a time of joy and a time of new knowledge. It is the necessary distancing from the event and the essential bridge into the day-to-day reality of ordinary living. But, like the honeymoon, it is for some a let-down or a time to face some of the implications and consequences and to raise newer questions. Honeymoons and mystagogy are sometimes traumatic, sometimes disturbing, at times an occasion for temporary grief over what was lost in making a choice. There are often mixed feelings during the honeymoon and during mystagogia: it can be a time of tears as well as a time of laughter, a time to face the consequences of making vows and permanent commitments.

But other analogues quickly surface in this exercise. Released prisoners of war or hostages have also had a heightened experience of mystery. They came face-to-face with death and have survived the ordeal. Upon release, there is that necessary period of debriefing and that slow reentry into the routines of daily life. There is that essential bridging time to name where they've come from and where they're going. There is a whole team of mystagogues from the medical world, a team of experts assigned to facilitate this "mystagogical" experience for them. And that team will not allow the POW's or hostages to put their experience on the back burner to be dealt with at some later date; it has to be dealt with now.

Another analogue for mystagogy is classical drama. The dramatist never leaves us at the climax but provides a period of unraveling called the denouement. Modern films will do the same thing for us when the story has engaged us in a mystery. *The Mission* is a good example. It never could have ended with the slaughter. There was a need to step back from that heightened experience and wind down before the lights were turned on in the theater and we were off to our "real" worlds.

Another way of getting in touch with mystagogy is the experience of having a child and finding oneself attempting to retell or articulate the meaning of bringing a new life into this world. Parents will further mention how that infant (read neophyte) altered their relationship as spouses and the relationships of the entire family (read parish community).

Some will name personal experiences that had a mystagogical dimension: their ordination to the priesthood, or the death of a loved one, or the time they moved away from home, family and friends. In each of those analogues there seems to be the very human need for taking some time after the event, to make time to remember, to be with loved ones, all in order to process the memory of all that has happened. They said that even the writing of cards helped them process some of the meaning of the mystery they had faced.

Mark Searle uses the analogue of teaching a child how to walk to get another insight into mystagogy.[3] There are no lectures to the child on how to walk, he says, but a person or persons who coax the child to move forward, to take the risk of letting go. These are people who know from experience that falls are not fatal, just some staggering, faltering and lots of picking up and starting all over again. It takes time to get someone to walk side-by-side with us; it never happens all at once.

I often relate the mystagogical aspect of discovering my roots. After my father died, my sister and I went to Italy to meet my dad's brothers and sisters, their children, all our aunts, uncles and cousins. Upon our return, we couldn't stop telling stories about that trip. It was a heightened experience of belonging and rootedness for both of us. I can remember that during one of those storytelling times my sister remarked that my story seemed better than the actual event. I was quick to respond: "Of course it is! The telling is the event remembered. The story is never just about the facts that happened, but the facts colored with meaning. The story tells others something about me as well as something about my father." We need to underscore that truth if we are to understand mystagogy.

It is only after such a hunt for common mystagogical experiences outside church settings that we can begin to name the unique and distinctive character of this fourth and final period of the initiation process. That is when we can make the connections and develop an authentic practice.

Here are some of the insights that come from our search for some analogues:

1. Mystagogy is not as mystifying as we first believed. It is such a normal and natural part of any heightened experience that the neophytes will do it with or without our permission. Our task is to facilitate a very natural experience. That is the first challenge of mystagogy for the pastoral team, finding ways to facilitate what is a very human desire after an experience of mystery.

2. Secondly, in each of the analogues we discovered the need to remember and relive the experience. Mystagogy is not a contrived practice to prevent dropouts or some antiquarian hold-over from a former period of Christian history. Remembering is an essential part of every heightened experience. The experience is incomplete without it. It is a time to discover new meanings, do some reflection, gain new insights.

3. There is need for a bridge between past experiences and the routines of our everyday lives. We learned that with our experience of the honeymoon and with the debriefing of the POW's and hostages. This is a time to be grateful and joyful as well as a time to wind down or cushion the shock of reentry.

4. The neophyte needs help with articulating the meaning of the experience. We got this insight from the experience of having a baby, the experience of teaching a child to walk, and also from the return of the hostages. A team of experts or specialists become the mystagogues who help us put words on the felt experience, who help neophytes learn the language of our tradition in naming their very personal experience. These "experts" do not allow neophytes to put off the questions and the feelings until some later date. We need people to surround the neophytes who have appropriated the paschal mystery themselves and thereby are able to encourage them to risk and to let go, people who have survived their own falls. The analogues teach us the need for guidance during the first and tentative steps of walking in Christ's way. Also, the telling of the event can sometimes seem better than the event itself.

5. Mystagogy is a time to make our very own the mysteries we have celebrated, a time to discover ways to make the big story our personal story, to give it our own stamp. The sacraments become ours and speak not only of who the Lord is, but who we are in relationship to the Lord and God's people. It becomes *our* exodus, *our* dying and rising, *our* salvation, *our* new life, *our* belonging and integration into the community. It is this personal appropriation that helps the neophytes to have the courage to give authentic witness to the story of Jesus as well as their own story of conversion.

6. We learned from the analogues that mystagogia is a time to face the implications and consequences of baptism. It is often a time of second thoughts, fear and discouragement. It is sometimes a traumatic and disturbing time, even an occasion for grief over what was left behind in making this choice, these vows and commitments.

7. We learned that mystagogy takes time. It does not happen all at once, but gradually. It takes time to follow in the way of Jesus and the way of

his people, this community. It takes time to learn about the mission, to learn how to evangelize, give witness and face the unredeemed parts of our world of work, family and culture.

8. We also learned that mystagogy is a community process. It is in community and not merely as individuals that we acquire the skills and courage for mission. It is in community that we deepen the meaning of baptism, confirmation and eucharist. It is in community that we celebrate the sacraments and live out their meaning. Neophytes change our relationships with each other in community as they come into our routines and the taken-for-granted of faith with new ideas, new awe and new energy.

9. The analogues also teach us that mystagogy is more poetic and imaginative than the other periods of the catechumenate. In attempting to describe the mysteries, we will run the risk of killing it. What D.H. Lawrence once warned about the novel should be taken to heart by us: "Beware of trying to nail it down. In doing so, you can kill it, or, worse, it may get up and walk away with your nail."

Now we are better able to read the paragraphs of the rite and understand more fully what it means when it says that mystagogy is:

(a) A time to deepen the Christian experience (RCIA 7).
(b) A time for spiritual growth (RCIA 7).
(c) A time for entering more fully into the life and unity of the community (RCIA 7 and 246).
(d) A time for making the paschal mystery part of their lives through reflecting on the Easter scriptures, sharing in eucharist and doing the works of charity (RCIA 244 and 24).
(e) A time for getting the help of the community to strengthen them as they begin to walk in the newness of life (RCIA 244).
(f) A time to gain a fuller and more effective understanding of the mysteries, a new perception of the faith, the church and the world (RCIA 245).

The process of mystagogical catechesis is not so much a scientific analysis and scrutiny of the initiation experience, but a deeper immersion into and reflection on the experience of the sacraments. It is not something outside the life and experience of the neophyte that needs to be learned; no, the neophyte is the subject that needs to be explored. It is others who have had the experience who can help the neophyte put a language on that experience.

I think it is unfortunate that the rite understates the gradual discovery of mission and ministry during the period of mystagogy. Obviously, a call to mission is presumed in article 245 with phrases like: "receiving the fellow-ship of the Holy Spirit," "a new perception of faith, of church and of the world." But I would have hoped for something stronger than "doing the works of charity" (in RCIA 244).

It is necessary to go to *The General Introduction of Christian Initiation* to discover that the reception of the sacraments of baptism, confirmation and eucharist "enable us to carry out the mission of the entire people of God in the Church and in the world" (2). It seems to me a great oversight that this paragraph did not find its way into the description of mystagogy in the rite itself.

All this exploration raises some issues about mystagogy:

1. If we don't have very good mystagogy in our catechumenal process, it could be not only that we lack understanding, but also that we've trivial-ized the mystery by the way we've celebrated it. If the vigil celebration was not a heightened experience of dying and rising with the Lord, what is there that needs to be remembered and teased out? The signs of the sacramental celebration need to be full and transparent. For example, submersion of the whole body at baptism is full of mystagogical possibil-ity, whereas pouring water over the candidate has much less mystagogi-cal content for exploration. An understanding of the paschal mystery of dying and rising with Christ is grasped experientially when one has gone down for the third time but did not drown. This is why article 17 of the National Statutes is clear in preferring total immersion to partial or to pouring. Likewise, if the dismissals have been practiced throughout the entire catechumenate, the neophyte has some fairly deep feelings to surface and name from that experience of being at the eucharistic table for the first time at the vigil.

   When the community takes time to call for an outpouring of the gifts of the Spirit and when confirmation is more than a hurried after-thought squeezed into the rite and rushed through because of time constraints, the neophytes will need the fifty days of mystagogy to. unpack that vigil experience and the experience of the forty days that prepared them for the celebration of the Sacraments. It will not be difficult to develop a sacramental catechesis when the sacraments have been experienced in an ample celebration. What needs to be remem-bered is that sacraments take shape in a process of encounter. They touch us deeply inside ourselves, they alter behavior and induce con-version.[4]

2. The vigil does not need to be re-hearsed. A hearse is for the dead and re-hearsing is twice as deadly, says Sam Keen in *Beginnings Without End.* The candidates and catechumens need to know very little before

the vigil. Most of all, we cannot tell them ahead of time how they're going to feel.

3. The parish community has an essential role to play during the period of mystagogy. The neophytes are the new statues, the living symbols that occasion revival and renewal for all the faithful. Therefore, it is important that the neophytes be seen and heard by the community during these Easter weeks. They "project their image" in the community; that is, they attempt to externalize in their behavior what has happened internally. The parish community is meant to come alive through this new birth in its midst (RCIA 246). As in the birth of a new child in the family, so also in the church: relationships will be altered because of the neophytes. The rite is clear about this and therefore suggests that the neophytes have special places during the Easter vigil (RCIA 248), that the community help its new members enter into its life and unity (RCIA 714, 244, 246), and that they be joyfully welcomed by oldtimers (RCIA 246). It is necessary to point out that bonding with the community does not mean that every neophyte will develop a friendship/relationship with all the members of the community. I once read that there is rarely room for more than eleven intimate relationships for any one person. Parishioners are not expected to become friends with every neophyte, but to move beyond acquaintances to companions with common goals, facing the same world with the same mission for the reign of God.[5]

4. Mystagogy is a bridge into ordinary time. We need to go back and reread the Acts of the Apostles, the first chapters of which are quite mystagogical. That well-known passage, Acts 2:44ff, beautifully describes an initial experience of faith where Christians loved, shared and experienced unity and the common life and where mission was practiced. But we do not have to go much further into Acts before we get into the story of the tensions, disappointments, suffering and errors that were part and parcel of ordinary daily living. We even learn about the backsliding and eventual dropouts in the story of Ananias and Sapphira. Ordinary Christian living is no Camelot. It is a struggle to live the gospel every day. Mystagogy provides a seven week period to come off the Easter high and onto the level ground of coming to terms with the reality of day-to-day faithfulness, learning how to do everyday liturgies, experiencing the lectionary for ordinary times, and learning how to do everyday kinds of prayer. These are the essential tasks to be dealt with during the period of mystagogy.

5. It is during mystagogy that the neophyte comes to understand what the rite calls "a new perception of faith, of church and of the world" (RCIA 245). The rite never elaborates the nature of this "new perception," but those who have walked this journey before know it to be not only the

kind of unfolding of meaning that Jesus does for the disciples on the road to Emmaus, and not only that new recognition they experienced in the breaking of the bread, but also a drive to give witness and to participate in the very message of Jesus. It is this sense of witness and mission that authenticates the conversion experience. Mystagogy must not only deal with the deepening of a religious identity but also lead to ministry and mission if it is to be authentic. Despite the poor example and countersign of the Bakkers and Jimmy Swaggert, we must admit that the Assembly of God does a much better ministry with its neophytes on this score than we Catholics do. Its neophytes come to understand the necessity of telling the good news to others. Without faithful testimony in the marketplace, faith becomes weak and dies. During mystagogy we must facilitate this witness and emphasize the missionary vocation of the Christian in the world of family, work, neighborhood and leisure. These are the primary places of worship. There, one is called to live a just life and to promote peace and make a preferential option for those who are treated unjustly in our society. Without this essential aspect of mission, conversion of hearts has been divorced from transformation of the world; the service we call them to becomes too churchy; they are propelled inward rather than outward. In short, we begin to clericalize the neophytes by trivializing ministry and mission into in-house code words. Mystagogy needs challenge as well as comfort. This sense of mission during mystagogy should come as no surprise to the neophyte. It should have been part of the discernment before the rite of election, and it should have been cultivated throughout the Lenten discipline.

Mark Searle, in updating the language of the third century criteria for readiness to begin Lent, translates the ancient questions as: "Have they come to appreciate the new justice? Have they learned to share their surplus? Have they learned to overcome the cannibalistic individualism of the age and put themselves at the service of the needy and oppressed?"[6]

I want to conclude with some pastoral ideas which help make all this practical:

1. First of all, designate early on several parishioners (or at least a coordinator) whose primary responsibility will be mystagogy. This is helpful since the parish staff and the catechumenate team are usually exhausted from planning and celebrating the triduum. This gives the staff a chance to be a part of mystagogy without having all the responsibility for facilitating it. The mystagogue is an imaginative kind of person who has the special skills of listening and naming; someone who is spontane-

ous, has lived the sacramental life deeply, who gives witness and is mission-oriented.

2. The Easter octave cannot be ignored. The neophytes must be urged to celebrate eucharist every day of their first week of Easter. I've always been surprised at how many of them really can do so, at either an early eucharist or an evening eucharist. They go to work an hour later than usual on these days. When this is impossible, they should be given the texts of the lectionary and directed to read and reflect on them day by day. We provide our own source books for the season with reflection questions, but there are some published versions available. During this week the neophytes hear more of the Easter stories and the first experiences of the church in the Acts of the Apostles. Models of new faith are exposed to them. They listen to the testimony of Peter and the other disciples. We hear about the insights and behavior of the Emmaus disciples, their struggle to understand and their willingness to witness. The neophytes' doubts get uncovered in the story of Thomas. Don't miss this critical week that springboards them into a desire for a seven week uncovering of their own sacramental experience.

3. Discover ways to highlight the neophytes at community celebrations, especially at the Sunday eucharist. Certainly they should wear their white robes or other identifying mark on the second Sunday of Easter. But they should also have special places in the community with their godparents. We give them a place next to the ambo in the first row for seven weeks. Perhaps an Easter symbol of some kind could be worn, but in some specific ways they need to be visible to the entire community.

4. The homily and general intercessions need to include references to the neophytes. There is no difficulty in referring to the neophytes since these Easter scriptures belong to them in a special way.

5. Perhaps the most important practice with the neophytes is also the most difficult—they must give public witness that springs from their own story of conversion. While it has not been easy for all of them to stand before the community after communion and speak for two to five minutes, we have found it is critical for our own renewal and their bonding. This is a safe place to do here at "home" what needs to be done out there in the marketplace. No matter how inarticulate, brief, fumbling and faltering that testimony may be, it works miracles for the neophyte and for the community. Let the extroverts go first; let the timid do it two at a time, if necessary; let them write out a brief witness statement they can read, but insist that all neophytes give some testimony.

6. We have found it necessary to schedule other times apart from eucharist when the neophytes and their godparents gather as a group during this seven week period. One of those times should be during the octave, preferably Wednesday or Thursday evening. The edited version of the Easter vigil video is shown as a stimulator for remembering. The neophytes and others show pictures, some personal experiences are shared, and the mystagogue does some sacramental catechesis off those stories. Of course, good fellowship and demonstrated love and unity prevail at such sessions.

7. Schedule a retreat day around the third or fourth weekend of Easter. The sacraments should be the focus of the retreat, but it is important to reflect on the link between liturgy and mission. Leonardo Boff's *Sacraments and Life* provides ample content for such a retreat. We have found that six hours on a Saturday with lunch together is convenient for the neophytes and adequate for quality time together.

8. The week before Pentecost should be devoted to a "novena" focused on the discernment of gifts, ministry and mission. If there is a stewardship committee in the parish, they can help with this. So often neophytes fall between the cracks simply because they were not registered when they entered the catechumenate, and therefore never received mailings and envelopes that kept them informed. It is not easy to link gifts to ministry, but every effort should be made to do so. No neophyte should celebrate Pentecost without some specific ministry for the coming year.

9. Link the neophyte to some subgroup in the parish for their neophyte year. Ideally, this is the same subgroup of the godparent. Ideally, it is also a small community in the parish that has a mission and is engaged in a specific ministry. Neophytes who have this kind of support do not become part of the high dropout rate in the first year.

10. Pentecost brings closure to the period of mystagogy. Do not treat it as an ordinary Sunday, but as one of the great feasts of the liturgical year. Celebrate gifts and ministries, especially those of the neophytes. Have a vigil of Pentecost that includes the reading of all the lectionary's optional readings. Pray for the outpouring of the Holy Spirit in the parish. Perhaps one of the parish prayer groups would want to be a part of such a vigil.

11. Lastly, do not neglect to celebrate the anniversary of the neophytes. It is easier to celebrate it during the Easter vigil than on a calendar date. We have found it helpful to ask all those celebrating their first anniversary to stand after communion at the vigil, then to ask all former catechumens to do the same. First year neophytes always provide the

party after the vigil for the new members. It is also a good practice to send an anniversary card by mail to last year's neophytes. The rite calls for some marking of the anniversary, even monthly meetings, which are critical if they are not linked to a subgroup. It also suggests a meeting with the bishop on his visit during the neophyte year (cf. RCIA 250, 251 and National Statutes 24).

And so we need to ask again: "Are you having any difficulty knowing what to do after the Easter vigil?" If you answer "yes," then join the crowd. All of us are working to become good mystagogues. If you are willing to "swim to Cambodia," name your own heightened experience of some mystery, and play all that out with someone else, I'm sure we'll be able to surpass Cyril's fifth century mystagogy and develop an authentic mystagogy for our own age and culture.

NOTES

1. *Egeria's Travels to the Holy Land,* John Wilkins, trans. Aris & Philips, Warminster, England, 1981.
2. I am indebted to Vince Connery, a great mystagogue, who helped put some words on this experience for me.
3. Mark Searle, "Mystagogy: Reflecting on the Easter Experience," Assembly, Vol. 9, No. 3, February 1983. Center for Pastoral Liturgy, University of Notre Dame.
4. Cf. Leonardo Boff, *Sacraments of Life, Life of Sacraments.* Pastoral Press, Washington, D.C.
5. Cf. *Growth and Intimacy in Small Groups.* Bob and Penny Fulton, Vineyard, Yorba Linda, California 92686.
6. Mark Searle, ed., *Liturgy and Social Justice.* Liturgical Press, Collegeville, Minn., p. 19.

Maureen A. Kelly

The Care and Nurture
of the Newly Initiated

What is "mystagogia"? Certainly it is not a household word among Roman Catholics. In true catechumenal style "mystagogia" needs to be understood from the perspective of image and story. The three stories which are told here encapsulate what mystagogia is.

Several years ago while having lunch with a young priest in Kansas City, the question of the dissonance of R.C.I.A. terminology came up. As I launched into a philosophical discourse about the symbolism of language and the fact that the unfamiliarity of the terms in the rite pointed to the fact that the rite was something very different than what we are used to in the church, the waitress approached our table. The priest turned to the woman and said, "Miss, have you ever had a mystagogia?" She paused, then responded: "No, but it sure sounds like fun." Mystagogia is like that. In its most pristine sense mystagogia is a time for rejoicing.

Around that same time, my brother and his wife who had been childless for sixteen years gave birth to a beautiful, healthy baby girl. Their barrenness had been a source of sorrow and pain not only for them but also for those who were close to them. The birth was a celebration for everybody. Upon my brother's return from the hospital he found a huge sign on their front lawn—"It's a girl!"—and in the weeks that followed there were letters, gifts, and phone calls from family and friends. All of us were excited about Megan's birth and the new life she brought to their marriage and to us. Mystagogia is like that. It is the excitement of the community over birth and new life.

These first two stories show in a small way what mystagogia is like for the community and the neophyte. They allude to the feel and the texture of this stage of the R.C.I.A. process. Images used to describe the initiation process are the images of falling in love and being married, of gestation and birthing, and as images are played out, this final formal stage is often referred to as, in the case of the marriage, the period of honeymoon, and, in the case of birthing, the period of growth and development.

The following excerpts from a neophyte's letter during her own mystagogia opens up another aspect of the neophyte's experience of this period,
that is, the tension and paradox that initiation and commitment lead to.

> Since you couldn't be with us, I thought I would write to let you
> know how wonderful it (Easter vigil) was. . . . I must admit that I
> was more than a little worried about being baptized by immersion
> but now I am very glad. . . . It was an incredible experience. . . .
> We are continuing to meet until Pentecost. I remember you saying
> that we would do that because . . . "you'll experience a lot of
> changes after Easter." I didn't really understand that then. I fig-
> ured that since I had already made the decision to be baptized and
> become a Catholic, I had already experienced my conversion.
> You were so right though. It's so weird and great, and very scary,
> but I do feel very different. I sometimes feel like I am going to
> explode! I used to have a hard time admitting to people that I was
> even going to the sessions, but now I want to tell the world! It's
> often depressing to find that the world doesn't always want to
> listen. Anyway, I am so glad that I can still meet with the others
> and ramble on about what is and has happened to me. (Letter
> from a neophyte, St. Rose of Lima Parish, Gaithersburg, MD.
> April 1988)

Mystagogia is like that, for the neophyte. It is a time of mixed emo-
tions, of great joy, because of deep conversions and of equal anxiety at
mission.

Mystagogia means an unveiling, or revealing of the mysteries. In practical pastoral experience it is the time when the neophytes unpack the
meanings of the rituals and conversion journey they have experienced.
Usually this occurs in the fifty days that follow Easter until Pentecost.
Parishes who take this stage of the process seriously plan ahead for it. The
major emphasis in this stage is still on Sunday when the neophytes gather
for the eucharist, continue to break open the word, and witness at these
liturgies as to what has happened to them. The formal period of mystagogia
also includes continued catechesis, particularly on the Easter sacraments,
using the Easter vigil as a starting point. The communal bonds which have
been developed during prior stages are also deepened not only through
liturgy and catechesis but through various celebrations.

And what happens to the neophyte on the Monday after Pentecost?
The same kinds of things that happen to people when "the party is over,"
when the newness of the baby or marriage wears off.

The fact that "the world does not always want to listen" becomes more real and daily than the memory of the Easter vigil. The care and nurture of the newly initiated cannot end with their "birthing." Just as a young married couple needs ongoing support when "the honeymoon is over," so does the neophyte.

At this point the stuff of this article deserves a comment. Practically and experientially across the country parishes have problems supporting, structuring, and sustaining a "short" mystagogia.

It is important for people who oversee catechumenal ministry in a local situation to ask why that is happening. In fact it is a moral responsibility not unlike the responsibility of the family to continue to care for and nurture the infant. Mystagogia, whether it is the formal time between Easter or Pentecost or a lengthier time, is dependent on what has occurred in previous stages. Where bonding and conversions have occurred when ritual and catechesis have been done in such a way that they open persons to meaning, they will bang down the doors for more. Parishes who do not have this experience with neophytes might want to look back at what has happened or not happened in previous stages.

To propose an ongoing structure in these situations seems at best overwhelming or practically impossible, and at worst unnecessary. Hopefully the reader is convinced that what could be done does not need to be overwhelming.

Before moving to structures and opportunities which can be developed it is important to review the assumptions or presuppositions which underlie them:

1. That there is a team, coordinator or committee whose major role and responsibility is to do mystagogia whether it is formal or ongoing. A lot of mystagogias slip into oblivion for the lack of energy of teams or individuals who want and deserve a break after Easter. It is interesting to note that sometimes the highest energy point for neophytes is the lowest for the team who has walked with them during the catechumenal stage.
2. The previous pastoral care and ministry with the neophytes has been such that the team and/or parish staff and leadership knows each individual well. Discernment is key at this juncture of the neophyte's life. Questions like "Where are the significant areas this neophyte will be living out his or her commitment to the mission of the church in family, work, profession?" "What kinds of support does he or she need for the development of his or her prayer life?" need to be asked.
3. There has been some bonding with the parish outside the catechumenal community.
4. That everyone knows the purpose of mystagogia, whether formal or ongoing, is to nurture, support, sustain and challenge the faith life of the

neophyte as he or she lives out his or her mission. It is not to create a
pool of "churchy" ministers, e.g., lectors or eucharistic ministers, and
then use that involvement as the criteria for connection.
5. The purpose of an ongoing mystagogia is not to add one more thing to
do onto what is probably an already fully packed adult life. Rather it is to
experience structures which meet needs expressed by neophytes.

An ongoing mystagogia is a commitment on the part of the parish to
provide structures and opportunities which intentionally provide care and
nurture of the neophytes as they deepen their commitment to life in Christ
and as they attempt to live out their conversion to a way of life based on
gospel values.

The type of structure will be based on the parish. All structures do not
have to be new. In fact, ideally, a parish will have existing groups and events
which will welcome the neophytes and which neophytes will enthusiastically
embrace.

Conversion means and demands a shift in values. It assumes a new way
of living. What is not always felt or sensed in the initial conversion of the
catechumenate is what it will mean to live this out in the day to day,
sometimes humdrum existence of what is real life. In catechumenal communities a lot of people care about an individual's conversion, new-found faith
and insights. Those people delight in watching the catechumen "fall in
love." Even when others are not interested or are blatantly hostile, there is
that weekly support and "place to come home to" as it were. As the
neophytes move into another phase they continue to need the support of a
group. Ideally parishes already have small faith sharing groups in place that
neophytes can choose or be invited into.

The first and central structure to look at for an on-going mystagogia is
small faith sharing groups, groups which focus on sharing the word/prayer,
or support groups. Some parishes fit this description—people who gather,
experience support, and share concerns and vision for living a Christian life
in the marketplace. Some of these groups do exist in parishes already and
neophytes should be linked with them by mutual agreement. Initially some
attention needs to be paid to communicating with the group on how to
include the new member and what might be his or her needs. At this
juncture in the neophyte's journey it is important to expand the community
he or she relates to. In other words, ongoing mystagogia does not take place
with the same group who have been through catechumenate together.
Neither is it a recycling of neophytes back into the catechumenate group as
sponsors or team members. There are parishes where R.C.I.A. thrives but
there do not seem to be faith-sharing communities outside of that structure.
In these instances the only viable approach is to begin with communities of

neophytes and former sponsors or other parishioners as facilitators. Ordinarily these groups meet once a month in homes.

Depending on the size and tenor of a parish these groups do not always have to be formal or have an agenda. One of the strongest and most positive experiences of incorporation into a small faith community which this author witnessed was that of Hazel, a retired neophyte whose sponsor was part of the daily mass group. The group had a Wednesday morning ritual of coffee at McDonald's after mass. Hazel became a part of that group, and it provided the support, challenge and witness she needed. This story also points out the role the sponsor can play in moving neophytes into ongoing groups.

There are times and places during the year to gather former catechumens and sponsors back together for prayer and reflection: anniversaries of rites of acceptance and election, Advent and Lenten reflections times. In the groups where retreats proved to be a valuable experience, it is not difficult to get a response from neophytes and sponsors to do it again. Besides retreats and experiences of prayer, many neophytes benefit from ongoing spiritual direction both one-on-one and in spiritual direction groups.

The team or person who oversees this stage is responsible to:

1. Know the neophytes.
2. Identify needs with the neophytes.
3. Keep in touch with them during the year.
4. Find groups in the parish that will provide "a place to come home to" or help develop them.
5. Link the neophytes to resources for deepening their prayer and spiritual life as well as on-going adult education.
6. Plan three or four activities over a year at which former neophytes and sponsors can gather.
7. Realize that everybody doesn't need everything or the same thing.

With these seven guidelines, an ongoing structure will provide for needs without being overwhelming.

James B. Dunning

Eucharist and Mystagogy— Goals of the RCIA from Kitchens of Lake Wobegon to Meals at Lake Galilee

That shy person of the airwaves, Garrison Keillor, speaks with fond affection of his mythical hometown, Lake Wobegon, "where all the women are strong, the men are good-looking and the children above average." With nostalgia he writes in his lonely apartment in the big city of St. Paul and laments his loss of community since those Lake Wobegon Days: "All those long conversations in vanished kitchens when for an evening we achieved a perfect understanding that, no matter what happened, we were true comrades and our affection would endure, and now our friendship is gone to pieces and I can't account for it."[1]

Apparently that nostalgia and need for community strikes many throughout our land. Several studies reveal that the first reasons why people join a church are: the influence of Christian people, family relationships and responsibilities, the search for community. They are all people reasons. In the past they came because of people and searching for people. Often we gave them books and lectures. Now we give them people. The "churchy" word for people is ministers.

There is a danger lurking in all this. If people join churches to get discipline and religion for their children or to get rid of loneliness in a groovy group, the church can wallow in warm fuzzies and get smothered in intimate cocoons. We would become a church of leaners and clingers rather than a church of missionaries. Remember, the Catholic church in Lake Wobegon is Our Lady of Perpetual Responsibility—response to God's gift by sharing the gift. Good ministers can help that happen. A woman told me, "I came looking for a better family, and I found a better God."

Therefore, since people come to join us for all kinds of mixed motivation, mostly valid but rarely adequate, ministers need to keep the goal of the

RCIA clearly in mind from the very beginning. I suggest the goal is eucharist. Another way to say it is that the goal is mystagogy—that marvelous Greek word for the fifty days between Easter and Pentecost. "Gogy" in Greek means learning, savoring. During Eastertime our new members savor the mysteries and enter more deeply into the mysteries of Jesus' dying and rising which they will do for a lifetime. They do that especially at eucharist; so, in a sense, eucharist and mystagogy are the same. We explore what that means for new members, knowing that what is true for new members is true for us all. The goal of all Christianity is eucharist and mystagogy.

RCIA Leads to Eucharist and Mystagogy

It all began with another group of people like us who discovered God at another lake, Lake Galilee, in another man who gave us far more communion than could happen even in the kitchens of Lake Wobegon. That man did not gather people in kitchens. He certainly offered few warm fuzzies or groovy groups. He did gather them at meals. Especially at those meals he was what theologians call the *primordial sacrament, the* image of God enfleshed in reconciling love. Those meals came to a climax in the last supper. There he promised us his Spirit so that the church might become what theologians call the *basic sacrament,* the image of God enfleshed in reconciling love today. Since Jesus did that at meals, he commanded us to do that at meals—"Do this in memory of me." Therefore, a critical question is: what is "that?" What is the eucharist? Ralph Keifer (God rest him) once said that *the* criterion of readiness for initiation is hunger for the eucharist. For what do we hunger? Just bread and wine? What is the meaning of that bread and wine?

Eucharist is the goal of the RCIA, and all that we do from the first day when we meet inquirers until the Pentecost following their initiation we do in light of that goal. The RCIA says, however, that the catechesis of the period of mystagogy is the eucharists of the Easter season, in which the scriptures often ask, "Where is Jesus now?" (in the Spirit-filled community). In that sense, mystagogy and eucharist are the same. So we can phrase the goal in several ways. In the language of Vatican II, the goal of the RCIA for new Christians and the goal of all ministry for all Christians is eucharist as the source and summit of the Christian life. Again in the words of Vatican II, the goal is active participation in and from the eucharist. One of our staff members, Jim Lopresti, ministers with Catholics returning to the church. He insists that here also the goal is not just reconciliation and absolution from sin but eucharist. In his language the goal is that they become active apostles, witnesses, missionaries from the eucharistic table (not leaners and clingers). We are back, then, to the question: What is this eucharist?

The Big Lie

Jesus tells us: "Do this in memory of me." What happens when we do "this"? Whenever we do this, Jesus re-minds us who we are. We had forgotten who we were. We perpetrated the big lie—the lie that we are separate, worse—that we are strangers and aliens to one another.

It began at Babel. In our relentless quest for one-upmanship, upward mobility, I-win-you-lose, and cut-throat competition, like the citizens of Babel we build our mountains of pride. "Let's build a city with a tower that reaches the sky, so that we can make a name for ourselves" (Gen 11:4). Because everyone was grabbing for a name above all names, they began to babble. They could not understand each other. They were alien. Note that at the conclusion of mystagogy, the story of Babel is one of the readings for the vigil of Pentecost; and, of course the Pentecost readings include the story of people from Parthia, Media, Mesopotamia, Judea, Pontus and Asia all hearing the Spirit-charged disciples speaking their own languages (cf. Acts 2:5–12). The disciples began to put an end to all the babble.

The conversion Jesus preached assaults the big lie. Literally, he comes to re-mind us of what we forgot—that we are called to be one. The Greek word for conversion, "metanoia," can be translated "after-thought." How do we think-after, how are we re-minded after we hear the good news that we are not alien to each other?

Those who first heard the message refused to change their minds. The church leaders of Jesus' time chose amnesia and anaesthesia. Jesus tried to re-mind them and us especially at those meals. We can't understand last supper or eucharist outside the context of all those meals.

Jesus' Meals

In Luke, at major points of transition there is a meal. Look at some of the characters who get into those meals. There is that woman "who had a bad name in the town" kissing and washing his feet with her tears and anointing them with perfume (cf. Lk 7:36–50). Those are all eucharistic symbols. The New American Bible uses a less preferred text. It has Jesus say to Simon, the church leader, "Because she has loved much, she is forgiven much." The preferred text reads, "Because she is forgiven much, she loves much." Acceptance first, then love. Grace first, then morality.

That is how Jesus really tries to re-mind, change the mind of self-righteous Simon and us who think our perfection and towers of Babel earn salvation. Jesus reminds us we are to be one, all sinners, and all loved. At those meals he offers at-one-ment. Note, however, that Jesus does eat with Simon. If the Jewish leaders were upset that Jesus ate with tax collectors and sinners, might the latter be upset because Jesus ate with Pharisees?

There is the prodigal father, who breaks more rules of legalistic etiquette than the son (cf. Lk 15:11–32). All parents know that if their dissolute offspring signs away their lives on Visa, they ground him for three weeks, take away the car keys, and unplug the stereo. This addlepated old fool is just waiting to stumble down the road, embrace the kid, ring his finger, cloak his body, and throw a party with prime rib at Antoine's of Galilee.

There is that wretched shrimp, Zacchaeus the tax collector for the Romans (cf. Lk 19:1–10). He is the Walker brothers of his day, traitor, guilty of treason. Yet Jesus says, "Let's chow down at your place." The ultimate compliment for a Jew was to eat at "your place."

Note that both the prodigal son and Zacchaeus are probably presented by Luke not just as individuals but as symbols of the outsiders who, like the Gentiles, dealt with pigs, seen as unclean by the Jews. The son was taking care of pigs, and the form of tax for the collectors was often pigs.

Luke brings all this to a climax at Emmaus (cf. Lk 24:13–35). Two dejected disciples are still asking, "Why do bad things happen to good people?" Jesus re-minds them on the road that thus it has ever been for Moses and all the prophets in non-prophet organizations. Grace is only grace and gift when we are ungifted. God can only fill the empty, empower the powerless, heal the broken. They are finally re-minded. They discover Jesus' presence in the breaking of the bread, not just the bread but the shared brokenness, "my body *given* for you." Jesus disappears in one body but remains with us in his new body whenever we do *that* in memory of him.

Matthew is not so big on meals, but Frederick Buechner recasts his banquet story in these words: "God is the eccentric host who, when the country-club crowd all turn out to have other things more important to do than come live it up with him, goes out into the skid rows and soup kitchens and charity wards and brings home a freak show. The man with no legs who sells shoelaces at the corner. The old woman in the moth-eaten fur coat who makes her daily rounds of the garbage cans. The old wino with his pint in a brown paper bag. . . . They are seated at the damask laid table in the great hall. The candles are all lit and the champagne glasses filled. At a sign from the host, the musicians in the gallery strike up 'Amazing Grace.' If you have to explain it, don't bother."[2] Those who object have already made up their minds that grace cannot be amazing.

Mark's community was perturbed and objecting about too many people at the table—too many Gentiles (read sinners, outcasts, blacks, whites,
women, Poles, Hispanics, etc.). Scripture scholar Eugene Laverdiere suggests that when Jesus feeds the five thousand it is in Jewish territory and
only Jewish men eat. Then Jesus makes the disciples cross a stormy sea to
Gentile territory. He even walks ahead of them on the water. When he feeds
four thousand in Gentile territory, everyone eats—Gentile and Jew, female
and male (cf. Mk 6:30–52; 8:1–10). Mark is re-minding his community and
ours that the crossing may be "stormy" but we must get rid of the big lie.
Put an end to Babel. In Christ no one is alien. "There is no difference
between Jews and Gentiles, between slaves and free, between men and
women; you are all one in union with Christ Jesus" (Gal 3:28).

Scripture scholar Xavier Leon-Dufour insists that the last supper
gathers all these meals in two ways.[3] The synoptics and Paul offer one
tradition—Jesus' words: "This bread is my body broken for you; this cup is
the new covenant of my blood shed for you." If we are not re-minded, we
only recall part of that. Too much theology of the past recalled only bread
and cup as eucharist. We forgot that when we eat and drink that bread and
cup, *we* become body broken and blood shed for all those who feel alien
(Zacchaeus and all the prodigals of our times). We literally re-member; we
are members of each other in Christ Jesus. No more aliens. No more big lie.

John's gospel offers a second tradition. Because John knew that eucharist means *our* broken bodies and shed blood for the life of the world, doing
exactly what Jesus did at all those meals, he doesn't even repeat Jesus'
words. He has Jesus do what he always did at meals—wash feet, give his
life to re-member strangers into friends. "And if I, your teacher and Lord
have done that to you, what should you do for each other?" (cf. Jn
13:1–17). That is why washing of feet was popularly seen as a sacrament
until the thirteenth century. We sometimes made eucharist into things,
objects—bread and wine. Since John knew well what Jesus did at meals, he
never dreamed we would do that. He identifies not things but actions with
eucharist. Washing feet, breaking body, shedding blood make us one.

Forgetfulness

We forgot that very soon. St. Paul to the Corinthians: "I hear that
when you gather there are divisions among you. . . . When you assemble it
is not to eat the Lord's supper, for everyone is in haste to eat his own
supper. . . . Whoever eats the bread or drinks the cup of the Lord unworth-
ily sins against the body and blood of the Lord. . . . Those who eat and drink

without recognizing the body eat and drink a judgment on themselves" (cf. 1 Cor 11:17–34).

"Without recognizing the body"—back to amnesia and the big lie. Theologian John Haughey insists, "For Paul, Christ was inextricably the person of Christ-and-his-own-members."[4] Corinthians forgot that. They didn't forget who Jesus used to be. They forgot who he is and who they are. They forgot Jesus risen into his broken ones, recognized ("re-known") precisely in the breaking of us who are his body. They forgot that for Paul the image (doctrine) of the body of Christ is not primarily about church— ecclesiology. It is about Christ—christology. They forgot the Christ who makes us one and does away with the big lie of our divisions. Haughey notes, "Corinth was notorious for its ethnic antipathies, its exploitation of women, its rapaciousness, and catastrophic economic inequalities."[5]

Moving right along to the twentieth century, we have forgotten not only Jesus but his reminder from Paul. Liberation theologian Juan Segundo: "The eucharist brings people next to each other; it juxtaposes them. It does not make a community out of participants."[6] That's what happens when eucharist gets reified ("thingified") to just objects out there (bread and wine) rather than transformation in here (church as the basic sacrament, the living body and blood of the Christ). Eucharist becomes things, just bread and wine, if we forget that the community is the basic sacrament. The derivative sacraments are actions, actions of a Spirit-filled people—washing people into death and life, anointing people with that same Spirit, eating and drinking into communion with the Lord through God's people who *are* Christ's real presence. This is who Christ is and what Christ is doing here and now. If we forget that, the church as body of Christ becomes a kind of "appendage trailing the risen Lord from a distance."[7]

When we eat the body of Christ at eucharist, we become the body of Christ again broken for many, sent to wash feet. "The bread of life is both consumed and consuming. The eucharist is a dangerous food to eat, because it makes its consumers become what they eat. They become what they eat if they become bread for one another."[8] Not just the bread and wine but *we* are "trans-substantiated," changed into the body of Christ for the life of the world. We become other for others. If we forget that, eucharist becomes things, not a shared body. Instead of becoming us, eucharist becomes another commodity, an it, not a we.

Notice how our language perpetuates our forgetfulness and the big lie. We "attend Mass, see Mass, say Mass, assist at Mass, receive communion" as a thing rather than being one with, in communion with, acting in communion with not just Jesus but the body of Christ gathered in his name. In the name of renewal we even reduced "active participation" to actions of praying and singing with missalettes rather than actions of breaking bodies, shedding blood and washing feet. Some claim that many people don't need much of a catechumenate because they have been attending mass for years. Precisely! Attending. By osmosis they may have come to experience eucharist as the action of a people putting an end to the big lie. Or they may have seen the eucharist described by Segundo with people "next to each other, juxtaposed," still lying.

From that comes a whole parade of lies: worship without witness, celebration without service, liturgy cut off from life, supper without the washing of feet, and Jesus-and-me divided from Jew-Gentile, male-female, slave-free, black-white, Wall St.-Skid Row, cleric-lay, Anglo-Hispanic, east-west, north-south.

To Eat as Jesus Did

Jesus came to put an end to all those divisions. He did it especially at meals, so in a sense the goal of the RCIA (and of all evangelization/catechesis) is eucharist and mystagogia as imaged in those meals of Jesus. It is to eat as Jesus did. It is to gather at that kind of eucharist as source and summit of the Christian life, active participation in that eucharist which moves in and out through church doors. It is to become apostles and witnesses from the table, who enter more and more deeply into the dying and rising of Jesus, who recognize Jesus in the breaking of the bread—and *the* bread, the body, is ourselves.

If we know that, if this is the vision of community we offer which goes beyond the conversations in the kitchens of Lake Wobegon, then we shall surround candidates from the beginning of the precatechumenate with that myriad of ministers who are the church. They are the basic sacrament of Christ and the people of faith who witness to their relationship with God— evangelizers, ministers of hospitality, sponsors, godparents, catechists, presbyters, spiritual directors, social concerns ministers, catechumenate director, musicians, liturgists, fellow candidates, deacons, mystagogues, presiders, parish council and leaders, prayer companions, bishops, parishioners, the liturgical assembly—the body of Christ. The hook, of course, is that when we invite all these ministries into action, they themselves are living the eucharist, living as the body of Christ, extending the dying and rising of mystagogy. We hope that the candidates will come to say, "If we discover God's presence and love in all these people, perhaps we can be that presence and love." We surround candidates with sacraments of Christ that they might become sacraments of Christ. We prepare them for eucharist that they may become eucharist. We lead them to celebrate the dying and rising of mystagogy that they may die and rise for a lifetime and break bread with their sisters and brothers.

What are the implications of this for all ministry, all evangelization and catechesis? What if all sacramental formation surrounded children and adults with such a galaxy of ministers preparing them to be the body of Christ, active missionaries from the eucharistic table? What is the sacrament of reconciliation (Tertullian called it a "second plank," a second baptism), for returning Catholic became not just a privatized confession and forgiveness of sin but a return to active participation and from the eucharistic table? What if marriage preparation surrounded the couple with other couples who would support them and challenge them before and after their wedding day? What if Catholics came to understand that every eucharist puts an end to the big lie and makes us one in Christ's body and blood, broken and shed for each other? The RCIA raises such questions for all of us. As one priest said to me recently, after we raise such questions, nothing in the church can be the same again.

Conclusion

The community is the basic sacrament. But Catholics take the incarnation and sacramentality so seriously that we have all kinds of sacraments and sacramentals, smells and bells, when that community acts. "Where 'ere the Catholic sun doth shine, there's music and laughter and good red wine. At least I've heard them tell it so, 'Benedicamus Domino.' " That is apparent even to the casual observer in Lake Wobegon. I'll close with Garison Keillor's description of life at Our Lady of Perpetual Responsibility. He says: "[I was] tainted with a sneaking admiration of Catholics—Catholic Christmas, Easter, the Living Rosary, and the Blessing of the Animals, all magnificent . . . especially the Feast Day of St. Francis, which they did right out in the open, a feast for the eyes. Cows, horses, some pigs, right on the church lawn. The turmoil, animals bellowing and barking and clucking . . . and the ocarina band of third-graders playing Catholic dirges, and the great calm of the sisters, and the flags, and the Knights of Columbus decked out in their handsome black suits—I stared at it until my eyes almost fell out. . . . I wasn't allowed inside the church, of course, but if the Blessing of the Animals on the Feast Day of St. Francis was any indication, Lord, I didn't know but what they had elephants in there and acrobats."[9] It all began with another man with eyes open to wheat fields, fish in nets, fig trees, foals of an ass, birds of the air, lilies of the field near another lake in Galilee.

NOTES

1. Garrison Keillor, *Lake Woebegon Days.* New York: Penguin Books, 1986, p. 19.

2. Frederick Buechner, *Telling the Truth: The Gospel as Tragedy, Comedy & Fairy Tale.* New York: Harper and Row, 1977, p. 66.

3. Xavier Leon-Dufour, *Sharing the Eucharistic Bread: The Witness of the New Testament.* New York: Paulist Press, 1987, pp. 281–99.

4. John C. Haughey, "The Eucharist and Intentional Communities," in *Alternative Futures for Worship, Vol. 3: The Eucharist.* Collegeville: The Liturgical Press, 1987, p. 54.

5. *Ibid.,* p. 56; cf. Gunther Bornkamm, *Early Christian Experience.* London: SCM Press, 1969, pp. 151–52.

6. Juan Segundo, *The Sacraments Today.* Maryknoll, NY: Orbis, 1974, p. 10.

7. Haughey, *op. cit.,* p. 59.

8. *Ibid.,* p. 73. I am also indebted to Haughey for some of the phrases later in this paragraph.

9. Keillor, *op. cit.,* pp. 127–28.

Karan Hinman Powell

The Period of Purification and Enlightenment (Lent): Catechetical Sessions for the Elect (Years A, B, C)

Introduction

The following catechetical sessions are designed for those who have entered the period of purification and enlightenment, that is, the elect and the candidates for full communion who will proceed to the Easter sacraments at the completion of this Lenten cycle.

Recall that the Rite of Christian Initiation of Adults states: "The period of purification and enlightenment, which the rite of election begins, customarily coincides with Lent. In the liturgy and liturgical catechesis of Lent the reminder of baptism already received or the preparation for its reception, as well as the theme of repentance, renews the entire community along with those being prepared to celebrate the paschal mystery, in which each of the elect will share through the sacraments of initiation. For both the elect and the local community, therefore, the Lenten season is a time of spiritual recollection in preparation for the celebration of the paschal mystery. This is a period of more intense spiritual preparation, consisting more in interior reflection than in catechetical instruction, and is intended to purify the minds and hearts of the elect with a deeper knowledge of Christ the Savior." (RCIA 138 and 139)

Hence the nature of this period will be that of a forty day retreat, a time of spiritual preparation, a time of purification, and a time of enlightenment.

FIRST SUNDAY OF LENT— YEAR A: THE RITE OF SENDING OF THE CATECHUMENS FOR ELECTION AND THE RITE OF ELECTION

PREPARATION FOR THE RITE OF ELECTION

A period of time (two hours to an entire day depending on the group) should be allowed to fully prepare for the rite of election. This preparation is not a rehearsal of where to stand and what to say. Rather this preparation is a day of internal reflection on conversion. An outline follows for a three hour reflection time:

Introduction (about 5 minutes)

Review purpose of the day
Call to prayer

Gathering Prayer (about 30 minutes)

Song
Reading from scripture (a passage on desert or exodus would be appropriate)
Reflection on the reading (homily style)
Response song
Prayers of petition and hopes for this day
Song

Quiet Reflection (about 45 minutes)

Participants are provided with journal questions and scripture passages to assist their reflection.

The following questions are examples:

1. Identify the changes that have happened in your life, in your family, your work, your spiritual life, your relationships, etc. because of your participation in the catechumenate. Identify these changes in concrete descriptions as changes in behaviors, attitudes, relationships.
2. Describe the ways you have embraced the cross during these past months, years.
3. On the journey of the catechumenate identify the ways you feel you have wandered aimlessly. How have you journeyed in faith, in hope, and in love?
4. Identify the areas of your life where you still feel that you hold out—that you do not respond fully to the call of God and that you feel called to relinquish control during this Lenten time.
5. Choose one of the following scripture passages for reflection:

Exodus 15:22–17:7	The testing in the desert
Psalm 91	Security under God's protection
Deuteronomy 6:10–19	The testing in the desert
Deuteronomy 8:1–5	The testing in the desert
James 1:16–22	Response to God's gift

6. Answer the following questions:
   Which scripture passage most clearly articulates your hopes and fears for this Lenten time? Why?

Share (about 45 minutes to an hour)

Sponsor and candidate share with one another their reflections.

Large Group Feedback (about 30 minutes)

Catechist facilitates discussion or large group sharing based on the following questions/statements:
   About walking in the desert I have realized today . . .
   While walking in the desert these next forty days I hope . . .
   I fear . . . I dread . . . I expect . . . I long . . .
   I pray . . .
Allow enough time for all participants to reflect quietly and to share aloud. Interaction with one another is helpful.
   The catechist may want to conclude with a ten minute sharing on the meaning of Lent in the Catholic Church and the significance of this forty day retreat in the context of preparation for Easter and the Easter sacraments.

Closing Prayer

All recite Psalm 91 antiphonally. End with a song.

REFLECTION ON THE EXPERIENCE OF THE RITE OF ELECTION

Readings for the Rite of Election

> Genesis 2:7–9; 3:1–7
> Psalm 51:3–4, 5–6, 12–13, 14, 17
> Romans 5:12–19
> Matthew 4:1–11

When the elect or candidates for full communion and their godparents are gathered, the catechist first reviews the rites by using song or guided imagery, or by recapitulating the liturgical actions, or other appropriate means.

Journal Questions (about 20 minutes)

The elect and godparents quietly write personal answers to the following questions:

■ During the celebration of these rites, what did you hear/experience/feel that most touched you?
■ What didn't you hear/experience/feel that you had expected would happen?
■ What does it mean to be "elected" by God? What did you experience? How did you understand that experience? What are the implications of this "election by God"? What will it cost you now that you have said yes?

Allow time for the group to share with one another what happened to them both at the rite of sending and the rite of election.
Read the gospel aloud (Mt 4:1–11).

Individual Reflection Time (allow 30 minutes)

Reread the gospel (Mt 4:1–11). Jesus was led into the desert; we too are led into the desert to confront the demons of our hearts, of society, those alluring spirits which exist in the world in which we live.

Journal Exercise

Write a response to the following:

■ Which temptation of Jesus most speaks to you as a temptation in your own heart? Why?

■ Give a concrete example of how this temptation is made manifest in your life.

■ In what ways do you rationalize this temptation in your own life?

■ Are there favorite excuses, scripture passages, good sayings that you use to tell yourself that what you are doing is all right? List these rationalizations.

■ As you walk in the desert of this Lenten time are you willing to let go of the bonds of this part of your life?

■ What will it cost you to let go of it? Are you willing to pay the price?

■ Write a prayer asking Jesus to help you on your way.

Share (20 to 30 minutes)

The elect and sponsor spend time with one another sharing what they have written.

Large Group Feedback (allow 15–30 minutes)

The catechist facilitates a group reflection based on the following statements:

■ About Jesus' journey in the desert I realize . . .

■ About temptation and the power of evil I realize . . .

■ About my own journey in the desert of this Lent I now realize . . . hope . . . fear . . .

Closing Prayer

All recite the responsorial psalm for the day together (Ps 51:3–4, 5–6, 12–13, 14, 17).

SECOND SUNDAY OF LENT—
YEAR A

Readings

> Genesis 12:1–4
> Psalm 33:4–5, 18–19, 20, 22
> Timothy 1:8–10
> Matthew 17:1–9

Catechetical Session

Reflection: The catechist rereads Matthew 17:1–9, inviting the elect and godparents to listen to this gospel in light of the homily they have just heard.

Pause for a minute or two of silent reflection.

Journal Exercise (allow 10 minutes)

Invite the elect and godparents to write answers to the following questions:

1. In what new ways have you met God during these past months in the catechumenate?
2. Describe the experience of meeting God—where, through or with whom or what, how?
3. How did you feel going through the experience? How do you feel now?
4. What impact has this experience had on your life?
5. In light of this experience, what do you think "the transfiguration" means? What does it mean to you?
6. In what ways do you still long to meet God? In what ways do you hope to be transformed?

Small Group Sharing (30 minutes)

Form small groups of six (elect and godparents participate in the same small group together).

Large Group Feedback

Catechist calls together all the groups to share with one another. Discussion focuses on the following questions:

1. What is the meaning of the transfiguration? For each one personally? for the church?
2. What is the significance of this reading for the Lenten time? for the period of purification and enlightenment?

PREPARATION FOR FIRST SCRUTINY

The last twenty minutes of the catechetical session should be devoted to preparation for the first scrutiny next Sunday.

1. Briefly explain what "scrutiny" is and what it is not. It is "taking a deep hard look." It is not "pointing fingers!"
2. Invite the elect and godparents to pause and reflect quietly for a moment on where they experience thirst—longing for God, in themselves, in the church, in the world.
3. Invite the elect and godparents to briefly identify (through a brainstorming process):

■ places in the world or situations in the world where they see, hear, or experience a thirst for God . . .

■ situations in the church (local and/or universal) which thirst for God . . .

■ places in their own hearts, their families, their homes where they long for God . . .

Note to Catechist: Include these ideas in the prayers for the elect during the scrutiny in a litany form as a prayer for deliverance. In this way the Sunday liturgy of the word and the catechetical sessions are closely linked together.

4. As you send them away invite them to read John 4:5–42 for the next week and as they pray to ask God to quench the thirsts they have named.

Closing Prayer

Read the second reading: 2 Tim 1:8–10.

Using Prayer B of RCIA 102, bless each of the elect with oil.

Send them forward in peace and in hope with a song: "Praise God from Whom All Blessings Flow."

THIRD SUNDAY OF LENT—
YEAR A: CELEBRATION
OF THE FIRST SCRUTINY

Readings

Exodus 17:3–7
Psalm 95:1–2, 6–7, 8–9
Romans 5:1–2, 5–8
John 4:5–42

REFLECTION ON THE EXPERIENCE OF THE FIRST SCRUTINY

The catechist calls the group to prayer. A spontaneous prayer may be used or the prayer for the day. The catechist reads John 4:5–42 aloud.

Journal Exercise (about 10 minutes)

The elect/candidates for full communion and their godparents are invited to quietly reflect upon the following questions in their journals or in the silence of their own hearts:

■ During the celebration of this rite, what did you hear/experience/ feel that most touched you?
■ What didn't you hear/experience/feel that you had expected to happen?
■ What does the gospel of the woman at the well speak to your experience of thirst?
■ What are the implications of this gospel for you during this Lenten time? What will it cost you now that you have said yes to this word?

45

Share (about 10 minutes)

Allow a brief period for the godparents and elect to share on these questions.

Large Group Sharing Time (30–45 minutes)

Allow time for the group to share with one another in the large group what happened to them during the scrutiny: What happened? What did you experience? What touched you? What does this rite mean?

The catechist should briefly clarify the meaning of scrutiny, exorcism, and personal sin as questions arise regarding these terms and their implication for the celebration of the scrutinies.

PREPARATION FOR SECOND SCRUTINY

The last twenty minutes of the catechetical session should be devoted to preparation for the second scrutiny next Sunday.

1. Briefly remind the participants what "scrutiny" is and what it is not. It is "taking a deep hard look." It is not "pointing fingers!" We took a first look this week; we will look deeper next week.
2. Invite the elect and godparents to pause and reflect quietly for a moment on where they are blind—blind to the ways of God, in themselves, in their homes and in their families. Also reflect on the places where our world is blind to the power of God and seeks only power for itself.
3. Invite the elect and godparents to briefly identify (through a brainstorming process):

   ■ places in the world or situations in the world where blindness to the power of God exists (what isms block the ability to experience God).
   ■ situations in the church (local and/or universal) where blindness abounds (what isms block our seeing most fully).
   ■ places in their own hearts, their families, their homes where they are blind (what isms trap them).

Note to Catechist: Include these ideas in the prayers for the elect during the scrutiny in a litany form as a prayer for deliverance. In this way the Sunday liturgy of the word and the catechetical sessions are closely linked together.

4. As you send them away invite them to read John 9:1–41 for the next week and as they pray to ask God to reveal their blindness—the places they do not see—and that God indeed heal this blindness in them, in our church, and in our world.

Closing Prayer

Read second reading: Romans 5:1–2, 5–8. Close with a song: "Be Not Afraid."

FOURTH SUNDAY OF LENT— YEAR A: CELEBRATION OF THE SECOND SCRUTINY

Readings

> *1 Samuel 16:1, 6–7, 10–13*
> *Psalm 23:1–3, 3–4, 5, 6*
> *Ephesians 5:8–14*
> *John 9:1–41*

REFLECTION ON THE EXPERIENCE OF THE SECOND SCRUTINY

The catechist calls the group to prayer. A spontaneous prayer may be used or the prayer for the day. The catechist reads John 9:1–41 aloud.

Journal Exercise (about 10 minutes)

The elect/candidates for full communion and their godparents are invited to quietly reflect upon the following questions in their journals or in the silence of their own hearts:

- During the celebration of this rite, what did you hear/experience/ feel that most touched you?
- What didn't you hear/experience/feel that you had expected would happen?
- How does the gospel of the man born blind speak to your experience of blindness? With which character did you most identify in the gospel? Why?
- What are the implications of this gospel for you during this Lenten time? What will it cost you now that you have said yes to this word?

Share (20 minutes)

Allow a brief period for the godparents and elect to share on these questions.

Large Group Sharing (30–45 minutes)

Allow time for the group to share with one another what happened to them during the scrutiny: What happened? What did you experience? What touched you? What does this rite mean?

The catechist then briefly clarifies the meaning of scrutiny and exorcism in light of social sin, social justice, blindness in our world, moral judgments and decisions.

PREPARATION FOR THIRD AND FINAL SCRUTINY

The last twenty minutes of the catechetical session are devoted to preparation for the third and final scrutiny next Sunday.

1. Briefly remind the participants what "scrutiny" is and what it is not. It is "taking a deep hard look." It is not "pointing fingers!" We took a first look with the woman at the well and personal sin. Then we took a deeper look at social sin this week with the man born blind. Next week we celebrate our third and final scrutiny in this time of purification and enlightenment—we call from the darkness of our hearts those areas that are in need of purifying. We call from the darkness of our collective heart as persons in a church and in the world to identify the bondage of sin that we with Christ may say no to sin forever.
2. Invite the elect and their godparents to pause and reflect quietly for a moment on where they are bound, where they are entombed, where they are not free in themselves, in their homes and in their families. Also reflect on the places where our world and our church are still bound and entombed. Include in this reflection the neighborhood, city, or town in which we live.
3. Invite the elect and their godparents to briefly identify (through a brainstorming process):

   ■ places in the world or situations in the world where people are still bound by death, by sin—where people are still entombed.

■ situations in the church (local and/or universal) where death abounds, where life is squelched, where women and men are bound.

■ places in their own hearts, their families, their homes where they are bound, unfree, trapped.

Note to Catechist: Include these ideas in the prayers for the elect during the scrutiny in a litany form as a prayer for deliverance. In this way the Sunday liturgy of the word and the catechetical sessions are closely linked together.

4. As you send them away invite them to read John 11:1–45 for the next week and as they pray to ask God to release the bondage they experience and reveal to them the ways they are called to unbind others and set them free—in themselves, in our church, and in our world, in our families, our neighborhoods, etc.

Closing Prayer

Read second reading: Ephesians 5:8–14. Close with a song: "What You Hear in the Dark."

FIFTH SUNDAY OF LENT— YEAR A: THE CELEBRATION OF THE THIRD AND FINAL SCRUTINY

Readings

> *Ezekiel 37:12–14*
> *Psalm 130:1–2, 3–4, 5–6, 7–8*
> *Romans 8:8–11*
> *John 11:1–45*

REFLECTION ON THE EXPERIENCE OF THE THIRD SCRUTINY

The catechist calls the group to prayer. A spontaneous prayer may be used or the prayer for the day. The catechist reads John 11:1–45 aloud.

Journal Exercise (10 minutes)

The elect/candidates for full communion and their godparents are invited to quietly reflect upon the following questions in their journals or in the silence of their own hearts:

■ During the celebration of this rite, What did you hear/experience/ feel that most touched you?
■ What didn't you hear/experience/feel that you had expected would happen?
■ How does the gospel of the raising of Lazarus from the dead speak to your experience of being bound, entombed, unfree? What words or images from this gospel spoke most deeply to you in this experience?
■ What are the implications of this gospel for you during this Lenten time? What will it cost you now that you have said yes to this word?

Share (20 minutes)

The godparents and elect share on these questions.

Large Group Sharing (15 minutes)

Allow time for the group to share with one another in the large group what happened to them during the scrutiny: What happened? What did you experience? What touched you? What does this rite mean?

Reflection on the Three Scrutinies (45 minutes)

Lead a discussion on the significance of all three scrutinies, reflecting on the process we have been engaged in during the past three weeks. In light of all three weeks how have they been changed, purified, enlightened? What new conversions of heart have they experienced? What new questions do they live with?

Note to Catechist: If necessary, briefly clarify once again the meaning of scrutiny and exorcism in light of personal sin, social sin, universal sin, social justice, the call of the gospel, moral judgments and decisions. Address any issues which are outstanding and in need of clarification.

Closing Prayer

Read first reading: Ezekiel 37:12–14. Close with a song: "Eagle's Wings."

PASSION SUNDAY

Readings

> *Matthew 21:1–11*
> *Isaiah 50:4–7*
> *Psalm 22:8–9, 17–18, 19–20, 23–24*
> *Philippians 2:6–11*
> *Matthew 26:14–27:66*

CATECHETICAL SESSION

Gathering Prayer

Call the elect and godparents to prayer. Lead with opening prayer for Sunday liturgy. Read Philippians 2:6–11. Pause for at least one minute of silence.

Quiet Reflection and Journaling (about 15 minutes)

Invite participants to journal on the following questions:

1. In light of today's gospel list five attitudes of Christ which struck you (these could be attitudes toward his friends, his accusers, God as his Father, himself).
2. In listing these attitudes describe what attracts you about each attitude and the way Jesus responded to others.
3. Of these five attitudes which one do you feel you most need in your life right now and describe why. What is happening in your life to cause you to long for this attitude?
4. In light of this longing what significance does the passion and death of Jesus offer to your life? What does this celebration of Jesus' death mean to you this year? How is this year different from all others? or is it?
5. What does it cost you to say yes to this paschal mystery in your life?

Read again Philippians 2:6–11. Pause for two minutes of silence to reflect quietly on this word.

Share (30 minutes)

Share in small groups of six (elect and godparents are in the same group).

Large Group Feedback

Call the group together for the last half hour to reflect upon the following questions:

- About Jesus' death and resurrection I now realize . . .
- About the cost of following Jesus I now realize . . .
- About walking the way of the cross I now realize . . .
- As I face this final week of preparation toward the Easter sacraments of baptism, eucharist, and confirmation I realize I must let go of . . . die to . . . embrace the cross of . . . fear . . . hope for . . .

Closing Prayer

Call to prayer. Read Philippians 2:6–11. Spontaneous prayers of petition. Closing Song: "Jesus."

HOLY THURSDAY

Readings

Exodus 12:1–8, 11–14
Psalm 116:12–13, 15–16, 17–18
1 Corinthians 11:23–26
John 13:1–15

Since the elect are dismissed throughout the triduum after the gospel, a brief session is provided for their reflection and nourishment during this time of final preparation for the Easter sacraments on Saturday evening.

Preparations

The catechist prepares the room with candles, the scripture being central to the gathering so that when the elect are dismissed they enter this room (this "upper room") of prayer and celebration.

Gathering Prayer

- Catechist invites the elect to pray.
- A spontaneous prayer is offered by the catechist.
- Read John 13:1–15.
- Invite the elect to share what they hear in this word that touches them this night. What does it mean for them? What is the cost of discipleship?
- The catechist then takes a towel, water, and a basin and washes the feet of each of the elect.
- Petitions: spontaneous, led by catechist or one of the elect.

Concluding Prayer

It is our duty to thank you, God our Father,
to sing to you, praise you, glorify you, exalt you,
bless you, magnify you and honor you

for the marvels accomplished for our ancestors in the faith and for us
    today.
You have led us from slavery to freedom,
from distress to joy,
from mourning to feasting,
from bondage to citizenship in your kingdom.

(St. Andrew's Bible Missal, p. 316)

GOOD FRIDAY

Readings

Isaiah 52:13–53:12
Psalm 31:2, 6, 12–13, 15–16, 17, 25
Hebrews 4:14–16; 5:7–9
John 18:1–19:42

Since the elect are dismissed throughout the triduum after the gospel, a brief session is provided for their reflection and nourishment during this time of final preparation for the Easter sacraments on Saturday evening.

Preparation

The catechist prepares the room with a cross, bibles, incense. The environment is stark and empty.

Gathering Prayer

Opening prayer for Good Friday service.

■ Read John 18:1–14.
Close your eyes. Imagine yourself in the garden with Jesus. What do you see happening? Describe Jesus' face. What is happening? What do you want to do in this garden with him?
Write your reflections.
■ Read John 18:15–18, 25–27.
Close your eyes. Imagine yourself with Peter, Jesus' closest friend and confidant. What does Peter feel? What would you say to Peter if you were with him?
Write your reflections.
■ Read John 18:28–40.
Close your eyes. Imagine you are in the praetorium with Jesus and with Pilate. Imagine Pilate's experience—how he felt, what he thought. Imagine

being with Jesus in that situation. What do you want to say either to Pilate or to Jesus about this situation?
Write your reflections.

■ Read John 19:1–16.

Close your eyes. Imagine that you are in the crowd. Jesus is scourged and crowned with thorns. You are part of the crowd that shouts: "Crucify him!" Pilate tries to stop your request by challenging you, yet still you persist: "Crucify him!" What are your thoughts and feelings?
Write your reflections.

■ Read John 19:16b–30.

Close your eyes. See Jesus on the cross. See the soldiers cast lots for his garments and offer him a sponge soaked in common wine. Hear Jesus cry out to his Father in heaven.

■ Read John 19:38–42.

Close your eyes. See the friends of Jesus take him from the cross, gently care for his body and place him in the tomb. Express to Jesus your hopes, your fears now of following him along this way of the cross. Speak to his friends (Peter, et al.) about their courage, about faithfulness in following Jesus. Ask them whatever question or concern is in your heart.
Write your reflections.

Share reflections one on one with each other or in small groups depending upon time.

Closing Prayer

Offer prayers of petition. End in silence.

Karan Hinman Powell

The Period of Mystagogia—Year A Mystagogical Sessions for the Neophytes

Introduction

The Rite of Christian Initiation of Adults indicates clearly the content of the period of mystagogia. "This is a time for the community and the neophytes together to grow in deepening their grasp of the paschal mystery and in making it part of their lives through meditation on the gospel, sharing in the eucharist and doing the works of charity." (RCIA 244) During this period, "the neophytes are introduced into a fuller and more effective understanding of mysteries through the gospel message they have learned and above all through the experience of the sacraments they have received." (RCIA 245) "Since the distinctive spirit and power of the period of postbaptismal catechesis or mystagogy derive from the new, personal experience of the sacraments and of the community, its main setting is the so-called masses for the neophytes, that is, the Sunday masses of the Easter season." (RCIA 247)

The following catechetical sessions for the neophytes are built on their new experience as members in full communion, reflecting on this experience, on the Sunday readings of the lectionary, and all of this in light of our unfolding tradition as Catholic Christians.

MYSTAGOGICAL SESSION FOR EASTER WEEK BASED ON THE READINGS AND EXPERIENCE OF THE EASTER VIGIL AND EASTER SUNDAY MORNING

Easter Vigil Readings: Genesis 1:1–2:2
Genesis 22:1–18
Exodus 14:15–15:1
Isaiah 54:5–14
Isaiah 55:1–11
Baruch 3:9–15, 32–4:4
Ezekiel 36:16–28
Romans 6:3–11
Matthew 28:1–10

Easter Vigil Experience: Baptism
Eucharist
Confirmation

Easter Sunday: Acts 10:34, 37–43
Psalm 118:1–2, 16–17, 22–23
Colossians 3:1–4
1 Corinthians 5:6–8
John 20:1–9

MYSTAGOGICAL SESSION

Note to the Mystagogue: This session is best held walking through and in the places where the Easter vigil was held. During this session the neophytes are invited to experience and to remember the sounds, smells, sights, and experience of their initiation. Ask the neophytes to assemble where you first assembled that night of initiation.

The details of this session are difficult to outline since Easter vigil celebrations vary from parish to parish. It is up to the mystagogue (the one who is to lead this session) to adapt this session according to the rite you celebrated.

Invite neophytes and godparents to center themselves . . . by becoming still . . . to be aware of their breathing . . .

Invite neophytes to open their memories to receive all that their senses experienced—what they saw, what they heard, what they felt, smells they experienced on Saturday evening.

Creator God, be with us this night as we recall the great night—the celebration of death and resurrection in our midst. Open our senses, our hearts, our minds, our memories that we may savor the gifts you offered to us that night. Renew us in spirit that we may proclaim your praise through Christ our Lord. Amen.

The following imagery reflection will need to be adapted according to the ritual experience of the neophytes in each parish. What follows is a model or example of how to develop a suitable reflection. The directions "sing" are meant for the catechist or mystagogue (you may wish to invite a cantor to join you for this evening if you do not feel comfortable with solo singing of short refrains). The cantor could also play piano or guitar as background music for the guided reflection.

This guided reflection may take anywhere from thirty minutes to an hour. Allow ample time for the reflection. Do not feel as though all of it must be processed during this first mystagogical session. The period of mystagogia is a time to "unpack" the experience of the vigil. Tonight we provide the opportunity to remember and to recall the events of that celebration so that we can "unfold the mysteries" throughout the entire Easter season.

(Neophytes should have eyes closed, pen and paper ready.)

I invite you now to journey with me through Saturday into Sunday: Darkness . . . a small flame . . . grows . . . a large fire . . . blessed . . . a candle . . . (Sing) "Christ Our Light" . . . Journey in procession to the word. (Sing) "Rejoice, heavenly powers! Sing, choirs of angels! Exult, all creation around God's throne!" (Pause)

"In the beginning, when God created the heavens and the earth . . . God saw that it was all very very good" . . . (Sing) "Lord, send out your Spirit, and renew the face of the earth" . . . God put Abraham to the test . . . take your son Isaac, offer him up as a holocaust . . . "God said, 'Do not lay your hand on the boy . . . I know now how devoted you are to God . . . I will bless you abundantly.' " (Sing the refrain from responsorial psalm used at the vigil) . . . (Pause)

The Lord said to Moses, "Why are your crying out to me? Tell the Israelites to go forward. And you, lift up your staff and, with hand outstretched over the sea, split the sea in two" . . . The Israelites did as God commanded, they marched into the sea, the Egyptians following them. The Israelites arrived safely. The Egyptians drowned in the sea forever . . . (Sing the refrain from responsorial psalm used at the vigil) . . . (Pause)

"You who are thirsty, come to the water! You who have not money, come, receive grain and eat . . . Seek the Lord while he may be found, call him while he is near" . . . (Sing the refrain from responsorial psalm used at the vigil) . . . (Pause)

"Are you not aware that we who were baptized into Christ Jesus were baptized into his death? . . . This we know that our old self was crucified with him . . . If we have died with Christ, we believe that we are also to live with him . . . consider yourselves dead to sin but alive for God in Christ Jesus . . ." (Sing the refrain from responsorial psalm used at the vigil) . . . (Pause)

An empty tomb, women visit the tomb, lightning—a bright light flashes, an angel speaks: "Do not be afraid." The women leave the tomb to carry good news to others. On the way they see Jesus. "Peace . . . Do not be afraid . . . Go and carry the news to the others" (Sing gospel alleluia sung that night)

Invite neophytes to write (give sufficient time to write responses to each of the following questions)

■ What words or phrases, images or stories touched them that night?

■ What words or phrases, images or stories touch them now as they reflect on that night?

■ Describe the feelings they had as they experienced the light, the procession, the celebration of the word.

■ What meaning do they find in this part of the celebration for their journey toward the Easter sacraments? What difference does this make in their life?

■ What questions does this section of the liturgy raise for you about being a member in full communion with the Catholic Church?

Continue the Reflection

Invite neophytes and godparents to once again close their eyes. (Sing part of the litany of the saints as it was sung in your parish) . . . (Pause)

"In baptism we use your gift of water, which you, Father, have made a rich symbol of the grace you give us in this sacrament" . . . Bless this water . . .

"Do you reject Satan?" "And all his works?" "And all his empty promises?"

"Do you believe in God, the Father Almighty?" . . .

"Do you believe in Jesus Christ?" . . .

"Do you believe in the Holy Spirit?" . . .

"Those to be baptized please come forward" . . .

Remember the water . . . "N (say this for each name of each neophyte), I baptize you in the name of the Father and of the Son and of the Holy Spirit." (After each name sing the acclamation used during the celebration.) (Pause)

"Receive this baptismal garment . . . bring it unstained to the judgment seat" . . . remember being clothed in Christ . . . (Pause)

"Receive the light of Christ" (receive the candle offered to you) . . . (Pause)

Candidates for full communion, "do you reject Satan, and all his evil ways and all his empty promises?" . . . (Pause)

You who are to be received in full communion, "do you believe and profess all that the holy Catholic Church believes, teaches, and proclaims to be revealed by God?"

"The Lord receives you into the Catholic Church" . . .

"Be sealed with the gift of the Holy Spirit" . . . feel the oil as you are signed on the forehead with the cross . . .

Invite neophytes to write (give sufficient time to write responses to each of the following questions)

- What words or phrases, symbols or images touched them that night?
- What words or phrases, images or symbols touch them now as they reflect on that night?
- Describe the feelings they had as they experienced the litany of the saints, recitation or renewal of baptismal vows, pouring of the water or bathing, being clothed, the experience of receiving the light, of being anointed with the chrism in confirmation.
- What meaning do they find in this part of the celebration for their journey as Catholic Christians? What difference does this night make in their life?
- What questions does this section of the liturgy raise for you about being a member in full communion with the Catholic Church?
- From this experience define and describe baptism . . .
- From this experience define and describe confirmation . . .

■ What does it mean to be vowed? What do the baptismal vows mean for you?

Continue the Reflection

"You are now invited to stay with the body, the community . . . describe what you felt as gifts of bread and wine were offered at the table . . . recall the words of the eucharistic prayer, "This is my body given for you . . . take and eat . . . This is my blood shed for you . . . do this in remembrance of me" . . . (Pause)

Remember standing around the table . . . "This is the body of Christ"—receive it, eat it, become this body . . . "This is the blood of Christ"—receive it . . . drink it . . . become this blood poured out for others . . . (Pause) (Sing the refrain from the communion song[s] sung during your liturgy)

"Go in the peace of Christ, alleluia, alleluia (if this was sung please sing it here) . . . see yourself processing out of the church . . . members of this body . . . one body of Christ . . . in full communion . . . (Sing refrain from closing song) (Pause)

Invite neophytes to write (give sufficient time to write responses to each of the following questions)

■ What words or phrases, symbols or images touched them that night?

■ What words or phrases, images or symbols touch them now as they reflect on that night?

■ Describe the feelings they had as they experienced the liturgy of the eucharist, the offering of these gifts, the bread and the wine—taste and see—the recessional?

■ What meaning do they find in this part of the celebration for their journey as Catholic Christians? What difference does this night make in their life?

■ What questions does this section of the liturgy raise for you about being a member in full communion with the Catholic Church?

■ From this experience define and describe eucharist . . .

As time allows return to the room where the mystagogical sessions will be held. Have refreshments available and provide an informal setting, one that encourages storytelling, and invite the neophytes to tell the story from their hearts (not their papers) of what happened to them that night. Invite godparents to also tell the story. This storytelling is begun simply by inviting anyone who cares to speak to talk about what happened to them that night. (Time will go quickly!)

For next week invite them to bring their reflections on the vigil celebration so that we can explore more fully the sacramental life over the next weeks. Encourage them during Easter week to attend daily eucharist or to at a minimum read the daily readings since these readings are for them—the "neophytes."

Conclude with a prayer of thanksgiving (invite one or more of the neophytes to lead this prayer).

SECOND SUNDAY OF EASTER— YEAR A

Readings

Acts 2:42–47
Psalm 118:2–4, 13–15, 22–24
1 Peter 1:3–9
John 20:19–31

MYSTAGOGICAL SESSION

Opening Prayer

Let us pray.

God of mercy,
we no longer look for Jesus among the dead,
for he is alive and has become the Lord of life.
From the waters of death you raise us with him
and renew your gift of life within us.
Increase in our minds and hearts
the risen life we share with Christ
and help us to grow as your people
toward the fullness of eternal life with you.
We ask this through Christ our Lord. Amen.

Reflection

Read Acts 2:42–47 aloud. Reflect (invite neophytes to write or to reflect quietly) on the following questions:

1. What does this reading say to you about the Christian life? What are the essential components of this way of life according to Acts? How do you live these now? How would you like to live these in the future?
2. From your reflection on the Easter vigil about baptism and eucharist, describe your experience thus far of living this life. Define baptism and its

66

significance for this way of life. What part does eucharist play in this new life?

3. From your reflections on the Easter vigil in light of this reading what questions do you raise about life as a Catholic Christian?
4. What does it mean to you today to be a member in full communion with the church?

Sharing

Divide into groups of four to six persons and invite groups to share with one another reflections they have written. Encourage neophyte and godparent to remain in a group together.

Reflection

Read John 20:19–31. Thomas doubted that Jesus was risen. Many of us doubt that the vision of Christian community offered in Acts or which we desire can ever come to be. What word of hope, encouragement, faith is offered to you in this gospel? What does this gospel mean for you as you continue your journey and deepen in it with us? (Pause for a moment of quiet reflection)

Sharing

Invite small groups to continue to share with one another based on this question.

Large Group Feedback

Any insights may be shared about what you have learned about faith . . . about Christian community . . . about commitment . . .

Input

As necessary, input for about 7–10 minutes may be offered on the meaning of commitment and vows.

Closing Prayer

Read 1 Peter 1:3–9. Close with song, "Jesus Christ Is Risen Today."

THIRD SUNDAY OF EASTER—
YEAR A

Readings

Acts 2:14, 22–28
Psalm 16:1–2, 5, 7–8, 9–10, 11
1 Peter 1:17–21
Luke 24:13–35

MYSTAGOGICAL SESSION

Opening Prayer

Let us pray [in confident peace and Easter hope] (pause) . . .

Father in heaven, author of all truth,
a people once in darkness has listened to your word
and followed your Son as he rose from the tomb.
Hear the prayer of this newborn people
and strengthen your church to answer your call.
May we rise and come forth into the light of day
to stand in your presence until eternity dawns.
We ask this through Christ our Lord. Amen.

Reflection

Read Luke 24:18–35. Reflect (invite neophytes to write or to reflect quietly) on the following questions:

1. What does this reading say to you about faith, eucharist, carrying the word to others, about recognizing Jesus in others, expectations?
2. From your reflection on the Easter vigil about eucharist describe your

experience in light of this gospel where their "hearts burned within them at the breaking of the bread." What is the significance of eucharist?

3. The strangers went off to tell others about their experience; they did not protect it, nor did they run away and hide. Instead they went to tell others the good news. From your reflections on the Easter vigil and in light of this reading, how are you called to carry the good news to others in your family? your work? your leisure? your neighborhood? Who are the strangers to whom you carry this word?

4. In light of this reading, what does it mean to you today to be a member in full communion with the church? What is the cost of the vows you have promised?

Sharing

Divide into groups of four to six persons and invite groups to share with one another reflections they have written. Encourage neophyte and godparent to remain in a group together.

Large Group Feedback

Any insights may be shared about what you have learned about faith . . .

about Christian community . . .
about commitment . . .
about ministry . . .

Input

As necessary, input for about 7–10 minutes may be offered on the Eucharist and mission.

Closing Prayer

Read 1 Peter 1:17–21. Close with song, "Jesus Christ Is Risen Today."

FOURTH SUNDAY OF EASTER— YEAR A

Readings

Acts 2:14, 36–41
Psalm 23:1–3, 3–4, 5, 6
1 Peter 2:20–25
John 10:1–10

MYSTAGOGICAL SESSION

Opening Prayer

Song: "The Lord Is My Shepherd."
Prayer

Let us pray [in confident peace and Easter hope] (pause) . . .
God and Father of our Lord Jesus Christ,
though your people walk in the valley of darkness,
no evil should they fear;
for they follow in faith the call of the shepherd
whom you have sent for their hope and strength.
Attune our minds to the sound of his voice,
lead our steps in the path he has shown,
that we may know the strength of an outstretched arm
and enjoy the light of your presence for ever. Amen.

Reflection

Read Acts 2:14, 36–41. Pause. Read John 10:1–10.

Sharing

Invite four or five members of the parish community to come to share
with neophytes and godparents how they live as Catholic Christians faithful

to these readings. Each person invited to speak should be from a different walk of life (e.g., professional persons—doctor, nurse, teacher, engineer—factory worker, etc). Speakers should represent a cross-section of the parish. Allow each person five to seven minutes to speak. Invite them to reflect on the following questions:

1. In light of the reading from Acts what is the significance of your baptism today in your family, your work, your neighborhood involvements? In other words what difference does it make that you are baptized? How do you live out this commitment?
2. In light of the gospel, where Jesus states "I came that they might have life and have it to the full," where have you found life? How do you share this life with others in your everyday worklife? Please be concrete and specific in giving examples.

Reflection

Reflect (invite neophytes to write or to reflect quietly) on the following questions:

1. Name the ways you have felt most challenged or most affirmed by today's readings and the stories you have heard.
2. In light of this reading what does it mean to you today to be a member in full communion with the church? What is the cost of the vows you have promised?

Sharing

Divide into groups of four to six persons and invite groups to share with one another reflections they have written. Encourage neophyte and godparent to remain in a group together.

Large Group Feedback

Any insights to be shared about what you have learned about faith . . . about Christian community . . .
about commitment . . .
about ministry . . .

Closing Prayer

Psalm 23 (either sung or recited antiphonally).

FIFTH SUNDAY OF EASTER— YEAR A

Readings

Acts 6:1–7
Psalm 33:1–2, 4–5, 18–19
1 Peter 2:4–9
John 14:1–12

MYSTAGOGICAL SESSION

Opening Prayer

Song: "We Are Called, We Are Chosen."
Prayer

Let us pray [in confident peace and Easter hope that we might enjoy
   true freedom in walking in the way and life of Jesus Christ] (pause)
   . . .
God our Father,
look upon us with love.
You redeem us and make us your children in Christ.
Give us true freedom
and bring us to the inheritance you promise.
We ask this through our Lord Jesus Christ, your Son,
who lives and reigns with you and the Holy Spirit,
one God, forever and ever. Amen.

Reflection

Read John 14:1–12. Pause.

Sharing

Invite four or five members of the parish community to come to share
with neophytes and godparents about vocation, that is, about how they live

72

a lifestyle as Catholic Christians faithful to the gospels. Each person invited to speak should be from a different lifestyle (e.g. married couple, single person who feels called to single life, religious sister, priest, widowed or divorced person). Speakers should be an equal number of women and men. Allow each person five to seven minutes to speak. Invite them to reflect on the following questions:

1. In light of the reading from John what is the significance of your baptism today for the lifestyle you have chosen? In other words how is the lifestyle that you lead an extension or deepening of your baptismal vows?
2. Apply the following words of today's gospel where Jesus states "I am the way, the truth and the life" and then later states "The one who has faith in me will do the works I do, and greater far than these" to your chosen lifestyle. Please give a concrete and specific everyday example of how you live this message in your life.

Reflection

Reflect (invite neophytes to write or to reflect quietly) on the following questions:

1. Name the ways you have felt most challenged or most affirmed by today's readings and the stories you have heard.
2. In light of this reading what does it mean to you today to be a member in full communion with the church? What is the cost of the vows you have promised?
3. Define vocation and give one example of how you are called to live this vocation today. Be concrete and specific.

Sharing

Divide into groups of four to six persons and invite groups to share with one another reflections they have written. Encourage neophyte and godparent to remain in a group together.

Large Group Feedback

Any insights may be shared about what you have learned about faith . . .
about vocation . . .

about Christian community . . .
about commitment . . .

Closing Prayer

To be prepared by one or two of the neophytes. Be certain to inform them ahead of time so that they can prepare for this session.

SIXTH SUNDAY OF EASTER— YEAR A

Readings

> Acts 8:5–8, 14–17
> Psalm 66:1–3, 4–5, 6–7, 16, 20
> 1 Peter 3:15–18
> John 14:15–21

MYSTAGOGICAL SESSION

Opening Prayer

Song: "Come, Holy Ghost."
Prayer

Let us pray that God will open our hearts to recognize the
    movements of the Spirit (pause). . . .
Loving and gentle God,
by water and the Holy Spirit you have freed us from sin and given us
    new life.
You have sent your Holy Spirit upon us to help and to guide us.
Reveal to us this day the places where the gifts of your Spirit are
    lived out in our lives.
Show us where your gifts are made manifest and bear fruit—
your gifts of wisdom and understanding,
right judgment and courage,
knowledge and reverence,
wonder and awe.
We ask this through Christ our Lord. Amen.

Reflection

Read John 14:15–21. Reflect (invite neophytes to write or to reflect
quietly) on the following questions:

75

1. Define the following by using an example of each from your own life or the life of another significant person in your life:
   wisdom
   understanding
   right judgment
   courage
   knowledge
   reverence
   wonder and awe
2. Reread John 14:1–12 silently alone.
3. Where in your life right now is the Spirit felt to be present? Where do you feel the absence? What gift do you need most from the Spirit right now?
4. Return to your notes from the evening we reflected on the Easter vigil. What is confirmation? What was your experience of confirmation? What questions do you still have about this sacrament?

Sharing

Divide into groups of four to six persons and invite groups to share with one another reflections they have written. Encourage neophyte and godparent to remain in a group together.

Large Group Feedback

Any insights may be shared about what you have learned about faith . . .
   about the gifts of the Spirit . . .
   about commitment . . .
   about confirmation . . .

Input

As necessary, input for about 7–10 minutes may be offered on the gifts of the spirit and the significance of confirmation today.

Closing Prayer

Read Acts 8:5–8, 14–17. Invite godparent and elect to impose hands on one another in silence. Sing: "Come, Holy Ghost."

SEVENTH SUNDAY OF EASTER—
YEAR A

Readings

> Acts 1:12–14
> Psalm 27:1, 4, 7–8
> 1 Peter 4:13–16
> John 17:1–11

MYSTAGOGICAL SESSION

Opening Prayer

Song: "Come, Holy Ghost."
Prayer

Let us pray that we will recognize the presence of Christ in our
   midst (pause) . . .
Lord Jesus, in times of darkness and trial, desertion and aloneness,
you desire that we be about your work
trusting in your presence in our lives. Be with us in our hour of need
and in the hours of need of those who wander aimlessly without you
   or without community. We ask this in your name. Amen.

Reflection

Read John 14:17:1–11.

Sharing

Invite four or five members of the parish community to come to share
with neophytes and godparents about social justice and Christian action.

Each person invited to speak should be from a different type of work—not just those who do part-time work but those from your community involved in the peace movement, shelters for battered women or children, AIDS hospices or care facilities, prison ministry, alcohol or drug treatment centers, soup kitchens, etc. Find types of social justice or community action which are available for involvement in your town or neighborhood, or perhaps those which your parish actively supports. Speakers should be an equal number of women and men if possible. Allow each person 5–7 minutes to speak. Invite them to reflect on the following questions:

1. Tell the story, or a story, of the work that you do—the people that you serve and why you do this work.
2. In light of the reading from John what is the significance of your baptism today for this work you have chosen? In other words how is this work an extension or deepening of your baptismal vows?
3. What does John 17:1–11 mean for you in light of the work that you do?

Allow time for questions and answers upon completion of the presentations.

Reflection

Reflect (invite neophytes to write or to reflect quietly) on the following questions:

1. Name the ways you have felt most challenged or most affirmed by today's readings and the stories you have heard.
2. In light of this reading what does it mean to you today to be a member in full communion with the church? What is the cost of the vows you have promised?
3. Define discipleship and give one example of how you are called to live as a disciple today. Be concrete and specific.

Sharing

Divide into groups of four to six persons and invite groups to share with one another reflections they have written. Encourage neophyte and godparent to remain in a group together.

Large Group Feedback

Any insights may be shared about what you have learned about faith . . .

about discipleship . . .
about commitment . . .
about social justice . . .

Closing Prayer

Read John 17:20–26 as a prayer for neophytes and godparents. Close with the Lord's Prayer.

PENTECOST VIGIL AND PENTECOST SUNDAY

Readings for the Vigil

Genesis 11:1–9
Ezekiel 37:1–14
Joel 3:1–5
Psalm 104:1–2, 24, 35, 27–28, 29, 30
Romans 8:22–27
John 7:37–39

Readings for the Day

Acts 2:1–11
Psalm 104:1, 24, 29–30, 31, 34
1 Corinthians 12:3–7, 12–13
John 20:19–23

MYSTAGOGICAL SESSION

Opening Prayer

Song: "Come, Holy Ghost."
Prayer

Let us pray in the Spirit who dwells within us (pause) . . .
Father of light, from whom every good gift comes,
send your Spirit into our lives
with the power of a mighty wind,
and by the flame of your wisdom
open the horizons of our hearts and minds.
Give us courage to act with conviction,

to teach the gospel, to spread the good news.
Continue to work in and through us
in our families, our neighborhoods, our work, our world
to touch the hearts of others
through Christ our Lord who lives and reigns with you and the Holy
    Spirit,
one God forever and ever. Amen.

Reflection

1. Read Genesis 11:1–9.
2. Write or reflect quietly on the following question: What is the significance of Babel for today—in your family, your work, our world, our
   church? Where do we need the spirit of unity?
3. Read Acts 2:1–11.
4. Write or reflect quietly on the following question: What is the significance that the Spirit who unites tongue to tongue and person to person is
   already in our midst? What can you/I/we do to recognize and listen to
   this Spirit more faithfully?
5. Read Ezekiel 37:1–14.
6. Write or reflect quietly on the following question: What is the significance of the dry bones for today—in your family, your work, our world,
   our church? Where do we need the Spirit of new life breathed into our
   bones? What gifts do we need in our church and in our world to bring
   about renewal?
7. Read 1 Corinthians 12:3–7, 12–13.
8. Write or reflect quietly on the following question: What is the significance that the Spirit who gives us all we need has already offered to us
   these gifts? Where are these gifts evident? What gift(s) do you offer?

Sharing

Divide into groups of four to six persons and invite groups to share
with one another reflections they have written. Encourage neophyte and
godparent to remain in a group together.

Large Group Feedback

Any insights may be shared about what you have learned about
faith . . .
    about the gifts of the Spirit . . .

about commitment . . .
about ministry . . .
about this process this year . . .

Closing Prayer

Read as a prayer to and for neophytes and godparents: John 20:19–
23. Recite sequence together (found in missalette). Invite everyone to offer a
sign of peace to each other in silence. Sing: "Praise God from Whom All
Blessings Flow" or "City of God."

Elizabeth S. Lilly

The Period
of Mystagogia—Year B
Mystagogical Sessions
for the Neophytes

Introduction

The reflections for the Easter Sundays and Pentecost are designed to
follow both the liturgy of the word and the liturgy of the eucharist. The
eucharist is the first response by the church, a response of thanks and
praise. When the neophytes and newly received gather, their reflections on
the word will be enriched by the great prayer of eucharist and communion.
The sessions depend on this.

There are, throughout the season, the constant themes of unity and
mission. The leaders, the mystagogues, will need to be attentive to the
particular men and women. There should be a balance between the invitation to remain centered in Christ and the church and the challenge to move
beyond one's small circle to bear the fruit of God's peace in the world.

There are no doctrinal or pastoral issues suggested for each Sunday.
Instead, there are the continuing and overarching issues of church, faith,
mission, service, charity, reconciliation, and hope. Again, the leaders are
encouraged to follow through with whatever is most important for the local
church. If the word has been broken open Sunday after Sunday during the
catechumenate, this process will continue naturally.

EASTER SUNDAY

Readings

Acts 10:34, 37–43
Psalm 118:1–2, 16–17, 22–23
Colossians 3:1–4 or 1 Corinthians 5:6–8
John 20:1–9

MYSTAGOGICAL SESSION

Opening Prayer

Sing an Alleluia! Select a hymn that you sang either at the vigil or at the Easter morning mass.

Reflections

1. Easter is the mystery of death and life. How do we approach this mystery?

   Tell your own story of the last few days. Then listen to the gospel of Easter morning again.

   In the gospel, the first visitors to the tomb, a place of death, could not understand what they saw. Understanding followed belief, and belief happened in the company of disciples. How many times have we not seen the significance of an event until we retell the story and see it again with new eyes? Who are the people with whom we tell the Easter story?
2. "Your life is hidden now with Christ in God." What does this mean? After your first eucharist, your first communion, you may not feel "hidden." Your celebration of union with the risen Lord is for God's glory. How will you uncover or discover this? When Christ appears, you, too, anointed, will appear doing good works, healing and reconciling.

   Today, recollect how the Lord has been revealed in your lives already. Share these moments of seeing and believing with one another.

Again, in the company of believers, our own faith grows, and we have insight and understanding.

Closing Prayer

The following prayer is adapted from the introduction to the preface for Easter. Invite all to name their own prayers of thanksgiving.

Leader: The Lord be with you.
All: And also with you.
Leader: Let us give thanks to the Lord our God, especially on this Easter day.
All: Individual prayers of thanksgiving.
Leader: We join all our thanks and praise with all the church and sing:
All: Holy, holy (or Alleluia).

SECOND SUNDAY OF EASTER— YEAR B

Readings

Acts 4:32–35
Psalm 118:2–4, 13–15, 22–24
1 John 5:1–6
John 20:19–31

MYSTAGOGICAL SESSION

Opening Prayer

The following is the alternate opening prayer from today's mass.

Leader: Let us pray
as Christians thirsting for the risen life.
Heavenly Father and God of mercy,
we no longer look for Jesus among the dead,
for he is alive and has become the Lord of life.
From the waters of death you raise us with him
and renew your gift of life within us.
Increase in our minds and hearts
the risen life we share with Christ
and help us to grow as your people
toward the fullness of eternal life with you.
We ask this through Christ our Lord.

All: Amen.

Reflections

1. The gospel tells of events of the day of the resurrection. Consider this Easter week. Recollect and share an incident or event that, to an ob-

server, would have appeared as ordinary and familiar, but that to you was new. Name a situation that was known to you, in your family or work, for example, but that you experienced in a new way. In other words, share an experience that had not changed from the week or month before, but that appeared in a new light to you.

Do you find that you describe your own experience with the same words that appear in today's gospel? Do you experience a peace?

2. "Put your hand into my side. Do not persist in your unbelief, but believe!" How is Christ present to us today? Christ is present in the broken bodies of the poor and the suffering. When we have doubts, like Thomas, and we do have doubts, we, too, need to put our hands into the wounds around us.

In our eucharist the bread, blessed and broken, becomes the body of Christ.

Where can we touch someone broken and suffering? Where can we allow others to touch our brokenness? In both instances, can we find the mystery of God's love made flesh, alive and present in our world?

3. The Acts of the Apostles records the care for the needy. What are the needs in our neighborhood? Who is addressing them? Where can each of us be more loving, compassionate, and forgiving today, and this week?

Closing Prayer

Reader: "A week later, the disciples were once more in the room, and this time Thomas was with them. Despite the locked doors, Jesus came and stood before them. 'Peace be with you,' he said."

Leader: Peace be with you.

All: And also with you.

Leader: Let us share a sign of Christ's peace with one another.

THIRD SUNDAY OF EASTER—
YEAR B

Readings

> Acts 3:13–15, 17–19
> Psalm 4:2, 4, 7–8, 9
> 1 John 2:1–5
> Luke 24:35–48

MYSTAGOGICAL SESSION

Opening Prayer

The following is taken from the Easter IV preface.

Leader: Let us pray.
      O God,
      all-powerful and ever-living,
      we do well always and everywhere
      to give you thanks
      through Jesus Christ our Lord.
      In Christ a new age has dawned,
      the long reign of sin is ended,
      a broken world has been renewed,
      and we are once again made whole.
      We praise you with great joy.
All sing: Amen, Alleluia, Alleluia!

Reflections

1. We live with the continuing experience that everything is new and yet
   everything is the same. In the newspapers we can find stories of fear, of
   ignorance, sin and suffering. We find these in our own lives. Yet, like the

disciples in today's gospel, we can find the peace of Christ, the calm, exactly in looking directly into the brokenness of the world as they looked at the risen Jesus.

This is possible because of the community of faith, the community formed by the scripture, the love of God, the communion with the Christ in the breaking of the bread.

What are ways that the community continues to know itself and the Lord? Why do we gather for eucharist on Sunday? How is this a celebration of God's love, of reconciliation, of making whole what is broken, and of peace? How are we in continual need of the signs of Christ's presence and Christ's peace?

2. The challenge to the whole community is to reform our lives, to live in the knowledge of Jesus Christ. Examine the hungers of the world. Look into the hungry, those needing food, and love, care, and companionship.

Share with one another the fear of knowing too much and so being called upon to give too much. Encourage one another to act in addressing some of the hungers around us. Find out about local soup kitchens, placement agencies, homes for the suffering.

Closing Prayer

Leader: Let us pray as Jesus taught us to pray.
All: Our Father, who art in heaven,
           hallowed be thy name;
           thy kingdom come; thy will be done
           on earth as it is in heaven.
           Give us this day our daily bread;
           and forgive us our trespasses
           as we forgive those who trespass against us;
           and lead us not into temptation,
           but deliver us from evil.
           Amen.

FOURTH SUNDAY OF EASTER— YEAR B

Readings

> Acts 4:8–12
> Psalm 118:1, 8–9, 21–23, 26, 21, 29
> 1 John 3:1–2
> John 10:11–18

MYSTAGOGICAL SESSION

Opening Prayer

Give everyone a copy of Psalm 23 and invite all to pray together.

Reflections

1. Recognition of our need of salvation is important in our lives. Today we reflect upon the image of the good shepherd. Do we recognize this symbol? Do we need a symbol, an image to recognize in order to know who we ourselves are, to know to whom we belong, to know where we are going? Where do I recognize my need for a guide, and where do I realize my own potential to lead?

   How is the church recognized today as a shepherd, as a loving caretaker and guide, a protector from evil? How familiar are you with the social action messages of the popes of this century, or the letters of the United States bishops on peace and economic justice, for example?

   On the other side of the image of the good shepherd, how do each of us, members of the body of Christ, image this symbol to others in our lives? In other words, how well or where and when do we recognize a need for healing, for nourishment, that we can begin to fill?

2. Where today do we hear the sound of the voice of the Lord? Throughout these Easter days we hear again and again the sound of the word

"peace." This may come as a prayer, as a cry for security, a wish, a plea. It may be whispered or printed in a headline.

In the communion rite, we turn to one another and exchange the sign of the Lord's peace. Do we understand this as the Lord's Easter prayer to us that we the faithful in turn are empowered to give and receive from one another? How prayerful are we in this moment of communion? What other times do we, the church, return to our common story, our common faith, to hear the sound of his voice?

Reflect for some moments on any number of times throughout the day or week when we have the opportunity to hear the word of peace. How is it spoken—as an invitation, affirmation, trust, patience, time? When have I heard it? When do I need to be more attentive to hear it? When have I spoken it? When do I need to be more conscious of my need to speak it? What will I do this week to echo the sound of peace in the world?

Closing Prayer

Sing a hymn known in your parish that recognizes the church in the good shepherd.

FIFTH SUNDAY OF EASTER— YEAR B

Readings

Acts 9:26–31
Psalm 22:26–27, 28, 30, 31–32
1 John 3:18–24
John 15:1–8

MYSTAGOGICAL SESSION

Opening Prayer

Invite everyone to hold hands with one another and pray the Lord's prayer.

Reflections

1. The three readings today present a vivid image of the organic nature of discipleship. To be a follower of the Lord is to be in communion with the word of God, to be at peace and filled with the Spirit, and to bear fruit. This calls for nourishment, connectedness, evaluation and reflection, and continual alteration—in other words, a continual conversion to the will of God.

   In seeking to understand the will of God in our lives, each of us is in relationship with the word of God, the company of believers, and the world in which we live. Share the experience of these Easter Sundays of liturgy. The celebration of eucharist is a prayer for unity and a sign of unity. The dismissal charges us to "go to love and serve the Lord." How do we become agents of unity in our world?

2. One of the promises of the union with God's truth is the presence of the Spirit. How do we know and experience this presence, this grace? Review several passages from the readings: "making steady progress in

the fear of the Lord," "increased consolation of the Holy Spirit," "from the Spirit that he gave us" and so on. All of these have to do with our openness to doing God's will.

That we gather to hear the word, to give thanks, to pray for unity in communion with the church, the faithful, are all signs of the Spirit's presence. We are responding to God's invitation, God's initiative in loving us. Share this idea, express it in your own words, let it sink into your heart. The Spirit calls us to be church.

3. The fullness of our union with God, with God's will, with the church, as the body of Christ is expressed in today's gospel as the fruit of the vine. We are called to be church not for our own comfort and wholeness, but for the world. Like a vine, we are growing. Likewise we need tending, pruning, and training. Each one can examine his or her own life and find an aspect that needs to become more fruitful. This can be recorded in a journal or shared.

Closing Prayer

Leader: Let us pray.
         Take a few moments to examine your life. Recall that for which you are thankful and grateful. Discover that which needs new direction and grace. When I invite you, please speak your prayer in a few words.

         Almighty God,
         for your grace and truth we are thankful,
         for . . .
All: (individual prayers)
Leader: For your constant love, we thank you.
         For our needs we pray. . . .
All: (individual prayers)
Leader: Loving God, we pray in the name of Jesus Christ, your Son, our Lord.
All: Amen.

SIXTH SUNDAY OF EASTER— YEAR B

Readings

Acts 10:25–26, 34–35, 44–48
Psalm 98:1, 2–3, 3–4
1 John 4:7–10
John 15:9–17

MYSTAGOGICAL SESSION

Opening Prayer

Invite all to pray together the Act of Charity.

Leader: Let us pray.
All: O my God,
        I love you above all things,
        with my whole heart and soul,
        because you are all good
        and worthy of my love.
        I love my neighbor as myself for the love of you.
        I forgive all who have injured me
        and I ask pardon of all whom I have injured.
        Amen.

Reflections

1. Today we continue to have the image of "bearing fruit" brought out in the gospel. This is the evidence of our cooperation with the love of God. What other ways do we image our unity with God? What are some of the advantages of the living, organic image of the fruit? Where, for example,

in your life has the maturing or ripening of a loving relationship or action taken time?

God's love is not static. God's love is an event, the incarnation, the life of Jesus. God's love is manifested in the anointing of the Holy Spirit, the christening, the Christ. How do we see the living, the birthing, the nurturing of this love in our lives and in the lives of others?

When are we more conscious of the absence of the signs of love, the fruit, the new life? What pruning can we do? What choices do we need to make to support life? If these choices are difficult, where will you turn. Remember the prayer of Jesus in today's gospel. Reread the gospel as a prayer with some particular relationship in your life in mind.

2. God's love knows no barrier; it is impartial. This is the ideal that we are empowered to reach. Share the areas in the life of your family or in society where barriers are dominant—race relations, economic justice, national and international security, power. The gospel, the whole Christian tradition, command us to act beyond these barriers.

How will we begin? Whom do we know who leads the way to love, peace, and justice in our own neighborhoods or in our nation or world? How will you join with them? What will you do?

Closing Prayer

Our eucharist is a prayer for union with God and for action to bring God's love to the whole world. Hear again the prayer after communion of today's mass.

Leader: Let us pray.
            Almighty and ever-living Lord,
            you restored us to life
            by raising Christ from death.
            Strengthen us by this Easter sacrament.
            We ask this through Christ our Lord.
All: Amen.

SEVENTH SUNDAY OF EASTER— YEAR B

Readings

Acts 1:15–17, 20–26
Psalm 103:1–2, 11–12, 19–20
1 John 4:11–16
John 17:11–19

MYSTAGOGICAL SESSION

Opening Prayer

The following prayer is adapted from the invocation of the Spirit from the confirmation rite.

Leader: All-powerful God,
           creator of all and Father of our Lord Jesus Christ,
           you send your Holy Spirit upon us
           to be our helper and our guide,
           to bring us peace.
           Open us to receive
              the spirit of wisdom and understanding,
              the spirit of right judgment and courage,
              the spirit of knowledge and reverence.
           Fill us with the spirit of wonder and awe
           in your presence.
           We ask this in the name of Jesus.
All: Amen.

Reflections

1. Who is the Christian, the witness of the resurrection, the believer? Each of the readings gives a portion of a description—one among the be-

lievers, one consecrated, one who knows Jesus, the Son of God, one who is filled with the Spirit. All of these enter into the truth of God's love for us.

Look at your own life this last week, these weeks of Easter, today. You are here among the community of believers, the church. How is the love of God present for you? As each one reflects on this, someone can reread the letter of John, aloud, with pauses.

What experiences of love uncover the presence of the Spirit? Where, on the other hand, are we more attentive to the urging of the Spirit and therefore more aware of the need for more loving action in our lives?

2. From time to time, we will not be able to maintain our commitments to be more loving. We will be more aware of our doubt, our isolation from the community, our failure to love. This is human. Return to the gospel, the prayer of Jesus. We of ourselves do not generate the Spirit. God's love is the beginning and the end.

Do not try to depend on your own resources in time of need. There may be temptations to do this. Do not lose sight of Jesus' prayer for us. Reread the prayer very slowly and thoughtfully.

3. We cannot leave today's readings without looking beyond ourselves, too. Situated in God's love and truth, the gift of God's Spirit, we are sent into the world. We continue to live.

With whom do we share our faith? How have our choices, attitudes, relationships changed? How has our world grown? Where do we know that we need to extend God's love—is there an area of ministry, of justice, of forgiveness where we need to begin to effect change?

Closing Prayer

The following prayer is from the Mass for Peace and Justice.

Leader: Let us pray.
        Lord, you give us the body and blood of your Son
        and renew our strength.
        Fill us with the Spirit of love
        that we may work effectively to establish
        among all people
        Christ's farewell gift of peace.
        We ask this through Christ our Lord.
All: Amen.

PENTECOST

Readings

Acts 2:1–11
Psalm 104:1, 24, 29–30, 31, 34
1 Corinthians 12:3–7, 12–13
John 20:19–23

MYSTAGOGICAL SESSION

Opening Prayer

Invite a musician to join you and sing a hymn that reflects the presence of the Spirit in the church, such as "One Bread, One Body" by John B. Foley, S.J.

Reflections

1. Today is especially a celebration of diversity in unity. The Acts of the Apostles and the gospel give accounts of the presence of the Spirit upon those who had witnessed the death/resurrection event. They are different in their details, but they express the same faith.

    Where in our lives do we see the need for inclusion rather than exclusion? Where have you experienced exclusion? Was it based on age, language, gender, class, culture, or something else? God's love is freely given and calls for inclusiveness. Where do we need to open our arms and lives to include those who have been excluded?

2. How do we hear the Spirit? The image of many languages yet one understanding is presented today. We communicate through all our senses, attitudes, and postures as well as the spoken word. What are we communicating in the language of conversion, the language of compassion, or the language of celebration? Examine each of these or the language that speaks most clearly in your situation.

    What has God accomplished and how do we communicate it? What is God accomplishing just now in you? What do you need to do to continue to cooperate with the Spirit?

Closing Prayer

The following prayer is from the communion rite.

Leader: Let us pray.
Lord Jesus Christ, you said to your apostles:
I leave you peace, my peace I give you.
Look not on our sins,
but on the faith of your Church,
and grant us the peace and unity of your kingdom
where you live for ever and ever.
All: Amen.
Leader: The peace of the Lord be with you always.
All: And also with you.
Leader: Let us offer each other the sign of peace.

Joseph P. Sinwell

The Period of Mystagogia—Year C Mystagogical Sessions for the Neophytes

Introduction

Easter is the centerpiece of Catholicism. During the Easter vigil and the sacred triduum, catechumens, the elect, their sponsors and the entire Christian community remember, recount and relive the death and resurrection of Jesus, savior and redeemer. The Easter season, from Easter to Pentecost, is the mystagogical season. This season provides the opportunity, especially for the newly initiated, to reflect on and integrate the call and mission to live daily as a disciple of the redeemer. Presumably, they will meet to pray, reflect and discuss once a week during this season.

These mystagogical sessions have the following parts:

■ **Proclamation** of the Easter season gospel in Cycle C and a period of silent reflection. It is presumed that these proclamations will be done in respectful prayerful manner and that the word of God will have a prominent place.

■ **Theme:** a brief description of a theme based on the Sunday gospel.

■ **Experiencing:** a group or individual reflection or activity relating to life experience.

■ **Praying:** prayer suggestions based on the theme will be offered.

■ **Exploring:** this section provides a series of questions or reflections and resources which develop the theme for leaders and the mystagogue. These questions or reflections can be used to organize a presentation or as discussion questions. If a video is mentioned, it is presumed that the video will be previewed. Most videos have discussion booklets; the discussion and reflections need to be adapted to the group meeting.

101

■ **Gospel Response:** provides questions which urge change in response to mystery of the gospels. A personal journal is recommended. At each session individuals can be asked to share their responses.

These parts are meant to be adapted to any sequence that best suits the group which is gathered in the parish. These are offered as starting points for mystagogical sessions.

The presumption in these sessions is that Easter focuses toward Pentecost and that the ministry of Jesus continues in the church. Each fully initiated person shares and is responsible for this mission. Each session will focus on the lectionary readings, primarily the Sunday gospel. Although these sessions are intended for the newly initiated (neophytes), other adults may find them to be beneficial.

EASTER SUNDAY

Readings

Acts 10:34, 37–43
Colossians 3:1–4 or 1 Corinthians 5:6–8
Psalm 118:1–2, 16–17, 22–23
John 20:1–9

MYSTAGOGICAL SESSION

Proclaim

John 20:1–9.

Theme

Mission To Save or Redeem. The resurrection of Jesus can serve as the starting point for reflecting on mission. Redemption means to buy back; by baptism we participate in the saving mission of Jesus.

Experiencing

Recall the Easter vigil as you listened to our story of salvation. Allow yourself to reexperience the water, light, oil, and your commitment of yourself to a saving God. What was your experience of being saved or redeemed? Have you ever experienced being bailed out or saved by another? (allow time for reflection and sharing in small groups)

Praying

Leader: God, savior and redeemer, you have freed us from everlasting death.

All respond to each prayer: By your cross and resurrection you have set us free; you are the savior of the world.

103

Leader: From everlasting sin . . . Response
Leader: From all evil . . . Response
Leader: From eternal death . . . Response

Exploring

1. What is redemption and salvation in the Christian tradition? What does it mean that Jesus is the savior and redeemer? How do I redeem the world and help save others? How is Jesus my personal savior and what are the implications for me and others? In light of salvation and baptism, what is the meaning of baptism and full initiation? How does each Catholic share in the mission of salvation and redemption. How am I in need of salvation? How do I help redeem others and the world?
2. View and discuss the video *Paul* from the Romans 8 Program (Tabor Publications) or the video *Resurrection and Ascension* from New Media Bible Series.

Gospel Response

Identify one person or group who needs God's saving power.
Identify someone you know who suffers from injustice.
How can you help that person?
How can you specifically act to alleviate injustice in your home, community or the world?

Some Helpful Resources

Sacraments and Sacramentality by Bernard Cooke, Twenty-Third Publications, 1983.
What a Modern Catholic Believes About Salvation by Tad Guzie, St. Thomas More Press, 1975.
Catholicism by Richard McBrien, Winston Press, 1980.
Stories of God by John Shea, St. Thomas More Press, 1978.
Before and After Baptism edited by James Wilde, Liturgy Training Publication, 1988.
An Easter Sourcebook edited by Gabe Huck, Gail Ramshaw and Gordon Lathrop, Liturgical Training Publications, 1988.
Resurrection by Morton Kelsey, Paulist Press, 1985.

SECOND SUNDAY OF EASTER— YEAR C

Readings

Acts 5:12–16
Psalm 118:2–4, 13–15, 22–24
Revelation 1:9–11, 12–13, 17–19
John 20:19–31

MYSTAGOGICAL SESSION

Proclaim

John 20:19–31.

Theme

Mission To Forgive. Jesus preached a gospel of forgiveness—unconditional forgiveness (e.g. prodigal son and woman in adultery). As Catholics, we celebrate the sacrament of forgiveness. We are challenged to forgive each other as God forgives us.

Experiencing

When did you experience forgiveness from another? What happened? Did you experience God in the act of being forgiven? How did you experience God? Allow for a period of silent reflection and invite individuals to share their story.

Praying

By alternating sides, pray Psalm 51 or Psalm 118—or pray together the Our Father while you hold hands.

Exploring

1. What is the Christian experience of forgiveness? What is the sacrament of reconciliation? What is the meaning of sin? Describe how the sacrament of reconciliation relates to your life and need for forgiveness. How are we "sacraments" of forgiveness for one another? How do I forgive those who injure me?

2. View and discuss the videos: *Pardon and Peace*, Teleketics, 1983 (12 min.); *My Son, My Son*, Franciscan Communications, 1987 (14 min.); *The Way Home*, Franciscan Communications (23 min.).

Gospel Response

Whom do I need to forgive in my life?
How will I take the first steps toward forgiveness?
How am I in need of forgiveness?
How have I failed in my relationships?

Some Helpful Resources

Sacraments by William Bausch, Twenty-Third Publications.

Putting Forgiveness into Practice by Doris Donnelly, Argus Communications, 1982.

Penance: A Reform Proposal by James LoPresti, The Pastoral Press, 1987.

The Wounded Healer by Henri Nouwen, Doubleday, 1979.

Understanding Catholicism by Monika Hellwig, Paulist Press, 1981.

Take and Receive by Jacqueline Bergan and S. Marie Schwan, Center for Christian Renewal, 1984.

Penance and Reconciliation by Patrick J. Brennan, St. Thomas More Press, 1984.

THIRD SUNDAY OF EASTER— YEAR C

Readings

Acts 2:14, 36–41
Psalm 23:1–3, 3–4, 5, 6
1 Peter 2:20–25
John 21:1–19

MYSTAGOGICAL SESSION

Proclaim

John 21:1–19.

Theme

Mission To Care. "Love one another as I have loved you." Caring is loving; it implies sensitivity, sacrifice and selflessness. Love is the greatest of the commandments.

Experiencing

When you were sick or in trouble how did you experience care? What characteristics were present?

Exploring

1. How does God care for each of us? What are the elements of Christian caring (cf. 1 Corinthians 13)? Describe them and offer examples. How does care involve risk, sensitivity? How does care involve compassion? Relate a story about caring for others or tell of a time when God cared for you.

2. View and discuss *A Way to God*, Part 3, Argus Communications, 1985 (20 min.) or *Martin the Cobbler*, Mass Media (19 min.).

Gospel Response

Choose one to reflect on. Who are the people in your family or community who need care, e.g. the elderly, the suffering, the lonely, the poor?

What steps will you take to care for them?

How can you care for at least one of them?

Consider the problems of the homeless, the hungry, the ignorant. How can you care for them?

Praying

The Prayer of St. Francis could be said together.

or

Leader:	For those orphaned by the lack of care
All respond to each petition:	God, deliver them.
Leader:	For the homeless
Leader:	For the hungry
Leader:	For the suffering
Leader:	For the poor
Leader:	For those who suffer injustice

(please add others who are not cared for)

Leader: We ask this in the name of Jesus who suffered, died and rose for all. Amen.

Some Helpful Resources

When They Ask for Bread: Pastoral Care and Counseling in Everyday Places by George Bennett, John Knox Press, 1978.

A Roman Catholic Theology of Pastoral Care by Regis Duffy, O.F.M., Fortress Press, 1983.

Spirituality Named Compassion by Matthew Fox, Winston Press, 1981.

When Life Hurts by Andrew M. Greeley, St. Thomas More Press, 1988.

Caring, Morton Kelsey, Paulist Press, 1979.

The Road to Daybreak by Henri Nouwen, Doubleday, 1988.

FOURTH SUNDAY OF EASTER— YEAR C

Readings

Acts 13:14, 43–52
Psalm 100:1–2, 3, 5
Revelation 7:9, 14–17
John 10:27–30

MYSTAGOGICAL SESSION

Proclaim

John 10:27–30.

Theme

Mission To Be Life Giving. Jesus came to give life—life everlasting. We are a grace-filled (holy) people. We celebrate God's life and offer God's life to others.

Experiencing

Reflect and share with one other person one of these questions: At the Easter vigil when you received the sacraments, did you have a life-giving experience? How can you describe it? Name or describe a life-giving experience. In retrospect how was the preparation for and celebration of your initiation into the Christian community a life-giving experience?

Praying

Leader: God, giver and source of all life, we give you thanks for your many blessings.

All respond to each phrase: "Thank you, God."
Leader: For faith
Leader: For ourselves
Leader: For our families
Leader: For our friends
Leader: For our country
Leader: For all creation
                             (*Please add your own persons or events that
                             you are thankful for.*)
At the end all say: Glory be to the creator, the redeemer and the
                             life-giver, world without end. Amen
                             Or
                             Pray Psalm 22.

Exploring

1. How are we a sacramental people? Why do we celebrate sacraments? Point out how the sacraments are ways of receiving and giving God's life. How is the eucharist a constant sign of God's giving life? How do we continue the life-giving dimension of the sacraments, or how do we bring life to others and the world? Reflect and discuss Jesus' statement, "My sheep hear my voice. I know them: and they follow me, and I give them eternal life" (Jn 10:27). Describe a life-giving experience. How have the sacraments been life-giving for you (offer examples)?
2. View and discuss *A Way to God Part 1,* Argus Communication, 1985 (20 min.) or *Right Here, Right Now,* Teleketics, 1981 (15 min.).

Gospel Response

Who is in need of life giving in our society? Identify someone or some group.

How can you bring life to this person or group?

How will this action demand change in your lifestyle?

Some Helpful Resources

Spiritual Journeys Towards the Fullness of Faith, edited by Robert Baram, St. Paul Books and Media, 1988.

Sacraments and Sacramentality by Bernard Cooke, Twenty-Third Publications, 1983.

Taking Flight by Anthony DeMello, Doubleday, 1988.

The Meaning of the Sacraments by Monika Hellwig, Pflaum, 1972.

Rediscovering the Sacraments by Brennan Hill, Sadlier, 1982.
The Book of Sacramental Basics by Tad Guzie, Paulist Press, 1981.
Doors to the Sacred by Joseph Martos, Doubleday, 1981.
Fully Human, Fully Alive by John Powell S.J., Argus Communications, 1976.

FIFTH SUNDAY OF EASTER— YEAR C

Readings

   Acts 14:21–27
   Psalm 145:8–9, 10–11, 12–13
   Revelation 21:1–5
   John 13:31–33, 34–35

MYSTAGOGICAL SESSION

Proclaim

   John 13:31–33, 34, 45.

Theme

   Mission To Be Witnesses of God's Love. "This is how all will know you are my disciples: your love for one another." Love implies giving and receiving. God so loved the world that he sent his only Son. We are the ones who continue God's mission. By baptism we are called to witness and serve.

Praying

   Reflect on 1 Corinthians 13:4–7 or Galatians 5:22–25 (Fruits of the Spirit). Allow the God of love to come to you and speak to you.

Experiencing

   Reflect on an incident when you knew you were loved. Who was present and what happened afterward. After or during your initiation how did you experience being loved? Reflect on how recently you have been witness to God's love. Invite individuals to share their reflections.

Exploring

1. Describe an experience in which you experienced God's love. What are the characteristics of Christian love or charity? What is the meaning and implication of the incarnation? Reflect on John 4:7–21. What does the call of Christian love demand and challenge from us in this century? Describe a person you know who is a witness of God's love.
2. View and discuss the video *Jesus' Bicycle,* Teleketics, 1984 (21 mins.).

Gospel Response

How am I failing to love? Ask forgiveness. How can I try to receive from others? How can I give to others, especially those who are poor and suffer? How can I volunteer my gifts or skills to help others?

Some Helpful Resources

The Cost of Discipleship by Dietrich Bonhoeffer, Macmillan, 1966.

To Act Justly, Love Tenderly, Walk Humbly by Walter Brueggemann, Sharon Parks and Thomas Groome, Paulist Press, 1986.

A Cry for Mercy by Henri Nouwen, Doubleday, 1981.

An Easter Sourcebook by Gabe Huck, Liturgical Training Publications, 1988.

Becoming a Catholic Even If You Happen To Be One by Killgallon, Shaugnessey and Weber, ACTA Foundation, 1979.

Love by Leo Buscaglia, Fawcett Press, 1972.

Portraits of Love by Daniel Berrigan, Crossroad, 1982.

SIXTH SUNDAY OF EASTER—
YEAR C

Readings

> Acts 15:1–2, 22–29
> Psalm 67:2–3, 5, 6, 8
> Revelation 21:10–14, 22–23
> John 14:23–29

MYSTAGOGICAL SESSION

Proclaim

John 14:23–29.

Theme

Mission to Peacemaking. God promises peace—a peace that surpasses all understanding. Pope Paul VI said, "Sow justice, reap peace." We are challenged to respond to the words of Jesus: "Blessed are the peacemakers."

Experiencing

As you listened to the gospel, what does peace mean for you right now? What experience of peace have you had in your life? Reflect on these words: "Peace is my farewell to you: my peace is my gift to you, I do not give it to you as the world gives peace." Share your responses with one another.

Exploring

1. How does sin prevent or damage peacemaking? What is social sin? What is a Catholic view of peacemaking based on the U.S. Bishops' pastoral letters "The Challenge of Peace" and "Economic Justice for

All." How do you view yourself as a peacemaker in your social responsibilities, e.g. citizen, worker, mother, father, wife, husband, friend? What does it mean in the twentieth century to call Christ "the prince of peace"?

2. View and discuss *A Way to God* (Part 5), Argus Communications, 1985 (30 min.).

Gospel Response

Talk with a member of your parish social action committee or volunteer to help at a food pantry. Examine your views on peacemaking and justice. What steps can you take to bring God's peace and justice to others in your neighborhood? How can you avoid consumerism? Read and reflect on one of the U.S. bishops' recent pastoral letters. Visit and volunteer in a soup kitchen or other social agency.

Praying

Repeat the gospel words "Peace is my farewell to you" and exchange a sign of peace with one another.

Leader: Let us offer one another a sign of peace.

Some Helpful Resources

Spirituality of the Beatitudes by Michael H. Crosby, Orbis Books, 1981.

The Rise of Christian Conscience by Jim Wallis (editor), Harper and Row, 1987.

The Challenge of Peace. God's Promise and Our Response, by the National Conference of Catholic Bishops, U.S. Catholic Conference, 1983.

More Than Words: Prayer and Ritual for Inclusive Communities by Janet Schaffran and Pat Kozak, Meyer and Stone Books, 1988.

Economic Justice for All; Catholic Social Teaching and the U.S. Economy, by the National Conference of Catholic Bishops, U.S. Catholic Conference, 1986.

SEVENTH SUNDAY OF EASTER— YEAR C

Readings

> Acts 7:55–60
> Psalm 97:1–2, 6–7, 9
> Revelation 22:12–14, 16–17, 20
> John 17:20–26

MYSTAGOGICAL SESSION

Proclaim

John 17:20–26.

Theme

Mission To Be One with Each Other. We are called to be one: that they all may be one (Jn 17:20). The four traditional signs of the church are: one, holy, catholic and apostolic. The church is the body of Christ. We are its members with a mission.

Experiencing

Have you ever experienced a sense of being bonded to someone or to a group? Describe the experience. How was God present?

Exploring

As Catholics how are we bonded to one another? As Christians how are we bonded to one another? What is the meaning of Christian unity? What is your experience of ecumenism or unity? What attitudes divide Christians from one another? Explore the meaning of the communion of saints? How are we joined to our brothers and sisters in other continents? How are you affected by your brothers and sisters in other countries? What does it mean to have a Christian global consciousness?

Gospel Response

How am I prejudiced toward others from different religions, cultures, sexes, educational or economic backgrounds? How do I promote these prejudiced attitudes? What do I do to change these attitudes? How do I see all of creation and humanity as part of God's creation and redemption?

Praying

Sing together "We Are in the Lord" or "There Is One Lord" from *Glory and Praise* Vol. 3, or pray slowly Philippians 2:6–11.

Some Helpful Resources

Declaration on Christian Unity, Documents of Vatican II.
Redemptor Hominis (Redeemer of Man), encyclical by John Paul II.
Models of the Church by Avery Dulles, Image Books, 1974.
The Faith of Catholics by Richard Chilson, Paulist Press, 1975.
Diversity and Communion by Yves Congar, Twenty-Third Publications, 1984.
More than Words: Prayer and Ritual for Inclusive Communities by Janet Schaffran and Pat Kozak, Meyer and Stone Books, 1988.
Community of Faith by Evelyn E. Whitehead and James Whitehead, Paulist Press, 1982.

PENTECOST

Readings

Acts 2:1–11
Psalm 104:1, 24, 29–30, 31, 34
1 Corinthians 12:3–7, 12–13
John 20:19–23

MYSTAGOGICAL SESSION

Proclaim

John 20:10–23.

Theme

Mission To Reconcile and Heal. Jesus healed others in a variety of ways. The death and resurrection of Jesus reconciled all of us to God. We continue the mission of Jesus to heal and reconcile if we are the disciples of Jesus.

Experiencing

Sin harms or damages relationships. How have you experienced this consequence of sin in your life? Identify one time. How was it caused? How did you experience God's healing?

Exploring

1. What is sin? What is communal sense of sin? Name some communal sins and why? How do we forgive others in community? How do we cele-brate healing and reconciliation? Describe how you will experience God's healing and reconciliation? Tell a story of reconciliation. Who needs healing and reconciliation in this community and the world? How

does the sacrament of reconciliation continue in our lives? How does the eucharist call each of us to reconciliation?

2. View and discuss the videos: *Healing Our Hurts*, Argus, 1985 (30 min.) or *Healing the Hurts of Intimacy*, Paulist Press, 1984 (30 mins.).

Gospel Response

Do I know someone who is in need of healing and reconciliation? What steps do I take to help this person? Injustice is a consequence of sin. It can cause human suffering, world hunger, homelessness, sexism and other social ills. How do I respond to these injustices? How can I help others who suffer from these ills in my own town or city?

Praying

There are many gifts but the same Lord. Invite each person to reflect on a gift that is God-given, and ask the Spirit to help each of us find ways in which to use these gifts to heal and reconcile others.

Pray the prayer: Come, Holy Spirit or sing "Come, Holy Ghost, Creator Blest."

Some Helpful Resources

Penance and Reconciliation by Patrick J. Brennan, St. Thomas More Press, 1988.

When Life Hurts by Andrew M. Greeley, St. Thomas More Press, 1988.

Healing the Eight Stages of Life by Matthew Linn, Sheila Fabricant and Dennis Linn, Paulist Press, 1988.

Whatever Happened to Sin? by Karl Menninger, Hawthorn Books, 1973.

The Road to Daybreak by Henri Nouwen, Doubleday, 1988.

The Broken Body: Journey to Wholeness by Jean Vanier, Paulist Press, 1986.

Morality and Beyond by John Westley, Twenty-Third Publications, 1984.

Notes on the Contributors

Rev. Thomas J. Caroluzza has been active in the adult catechumenate for fourteen years in four Virginia parishes. He served on the board of the North American Forum on the Catechumenate from its beginning until 1986, and has been part of its institute teams since 1980. Tom was also a member of the National Review Service Team for three years. He has authored more than fifteen articles on the catechumenate, liturgy and parish life, and frequently gives conferences and workshops throughout the United States. He holds a doctor of ministry degree and is currently pastor of Holy Spirit Parish in Virginia Beach, Va.

Rev. James B. Dunning, of the diocese of Seattle, is currently president of the North American Forum on the Catechumenate and consultant in parish renewal and formation. Father Dunning is a recipient of the John XXIII Award for Contribution to Continuing Education of Priests. He is the author of *New Wine, New Wineskins: Exploring the Rite of the Christian Initiation of Adults* and *Ministries: Sharing God's Gifts.*

Maureen A. Kelly is Catechetical Advisor for Silver Burdett Ginn Co. and chairperson of the steering committee of the North American Forum for the Cathecumenate. She has served as pastoral associate and director of the catechumenate in Gaithersburg, Maryland and Kansas City, Missouri. She holds an M.A. in theology from the Catholic University of Louvain, Belgium, and is the author of various articles and tapes. Ms. Kelly has given workshops throughout the United States and Canada.

Elizabeth S. Lilly is the liturgy coordinator and member of the catechumenate team for the five churches of Saint Thomas Aquinas parish in Palo Alto, California. For seven years she directed the catechumenate in Saint William Parish, Los Altos, California. During those years she contributed to the three cycles of *Breaking Open the Word of God* and more recently to *A Catechumen's Lectionary.* She has been a member of the liturgy commission of the diocese of San Jose and continues to serve on the committees on the catechumenate and environment and art. She is a graduate of the University of California with a master's degree in the history of art.

Karan Hinman Powell served for five years as executive director of the North American Forum on the Catechumenate. She is presently director of the Professional Development Program at Georgetown University. Past experience includes work with three parish catechumenates in Mississippi, Maryland, and Virginia. She is the author of *How To Form a Catechumenate Team* and co-editor of *Breaking Open the Word of God* for Cycle A, B, and C. She holds a M.Div. degree from the Jesuit School of Theology in Chicago.

Joseph P. Sinwell is diocesan director of religious education and co-director of the catechumenate for the diocese of Providence. He is a founding member of the North American Forum on the Catechumenate and served on its steering committee until 1988. He holds master's degrees in religious education and agency counseling and is a candidate for a doctor of ministry degree at St. Mary's University, Baltimore. Mr. Sinwell is co-editor of *Breaking Open the Word of God,* Cycle A, B and C.

Victoria M. Tufano is director of the liturgy office for the diocese of Des Moines. She received her master of divinity and master of arts in liturgical studies from the University of Notre Dame. She was a contributor to *Breaking Open the Word of God,* Cycle A, and has been a team member on Institutes of the North American Forum on the Catechumenate.